More than just a Brief attempt at Humor

ROUND 2

To Holly Rosenberg
With Best Wishes for
Good Health & Good luck
Bob Boxer
10-8-2013

Boxer's Shorts

More than just a Brief attempt at Humor

Round 2

Punchline Press
Wilmette, Illinois

CREATED BY ROBERT BOXER M.D.
ILLUSTRATED BY DARNELL TOWNS

Manuscript Editor
Carole Isaacs

Book and Cover Design
Darnell Towns/Robert Boxer/Chapter One, Inc.

Typesetting and Production Services
Chapter One, Inc.

Cover Illustration
Darnell Towns

Back Cover Photograph
Self-Timer

COPYRIGHT© 1994 by Punchline Press
All rights reserved. International and Pan American Copyright Conventions.
No portion of this book may be photocopied or reproduced mechanically, electronically, or by any other means without permission of the Publisher.

Published by Punchline Press
P.O. Box 6058, Wilmette, IL 60091

Printed in the United States of America

First Edition, July, 1994

Library of Congress catalog no: 94-092101
ISBN: 0-9620687-1-3

Contents

vi	Dedications
vii	Foreword
ix	Preface
1-121	Cartoons
123	Acknowledgements
126	About the Author
127	About the Illustrator
128-130	List of Cartoons
131	Book Order Form

Dedications

To the memory of John S. Crosbie, Chairman of the Bored, The International Save the Pun Foundation.

John passed away on January 10, 1994 at his home near Toronto, Canada. John had an illustrious career as an advertising executive in Chicago, and as the author of a number of books, including *Crosbie's Dictionary of Puns*. John was brilliant, creative, clever, and a kind person. He was dedicated to using humor, especially plays on words, to improving the literacy of the English-speaking world. John will be missed by all those who had the good fortune to know him.

To my wife Marsha and my sons Stephen and Richard for their patience in putting up with a punster husband and father.

Illustrator's Dedications

God has my eternal gratitude for endowing me with this special ability. To my family for their ongoing and ever-loving support and to my friends who have stood by me.

Foreword

FORWARD!

One of the things that made the book *BOXER'S SHORTS* unique was the way in which Bob Boxer worked with the illustrator, Darnell Towns, to create visual as well as verbal puns. In this new adventure into the world of word-play, Bob Boxer has continued to explore what happens when both the writer and the artist take pun to paper.

The appearance of this new book, *ROUND TWO*, will bring special pleasure to those who, having been entertained by his previous efforts, have been urging Bob Boxer to produce more. Their urging has been especially urgent ever since the International Save the Pun Foundation named him "Punster of the Year".

It should be noted that, to date, only six people have been so named in the history of the world. Even Shakespeare has been bypassed, a point that should bring pride to Bob Boxer's hamlet.

On behalf of the Foundation, we congratulate Dr. Boxer on his latest literary achievement -- and look forward to many more!

John S. Crosbie,
Chairman of the Bored,
The International Save the Pun Foundation

Preface

It makes me happy to see people enjoy the pun cartoons which I conceived and Darnell Towns illustrated. Many of my patients seem relieved to see that their doctor has a sense of humor, or at least, as some would argue, makes an attempt in that direction.

At times, I truly enjoy interjecting a humorous comment, particularly at lunch at the hospital with physician colleagues. Often my fellow physicians laugh, sometimes even sincerely, but after three or four attempts on my part, or with the first not so funny effort, they usually all leave, even if they haven't completely finished their meal. I rationalize this by thinking that I'm helping to prevent the health problems that may result from overeating amongst my physician colleagues. After all, punning is a legitimate way to get to the head of lines everywhere, and it's an equally effective means of establishing breathing space in crowded situations.

My real penchant, however, is not extemporaneous punning (there are hordes of punsters far quicker and much more clever than I), but rather the visualization of situations lending themselves to illustration as pun cartoons. I actually visualize the cartoon in its completed format. I'm fortunate to work with a talented illustrator who accurately draws my ideas.

All of the work that we create is original in the sense that I have not heard nor seen the humor previously spoken nor drawn. As I indicated in our first book, I suspect that no one can be aware of all that has preceded,

and surely similiar ideas must arise simultaneously. Original in this sense means not knowingly incited nor stimulated by the work or thoughts of others.

As with our previous works, I hope that our readers enjoy the blending of original humor and art that we have put together in this collection.

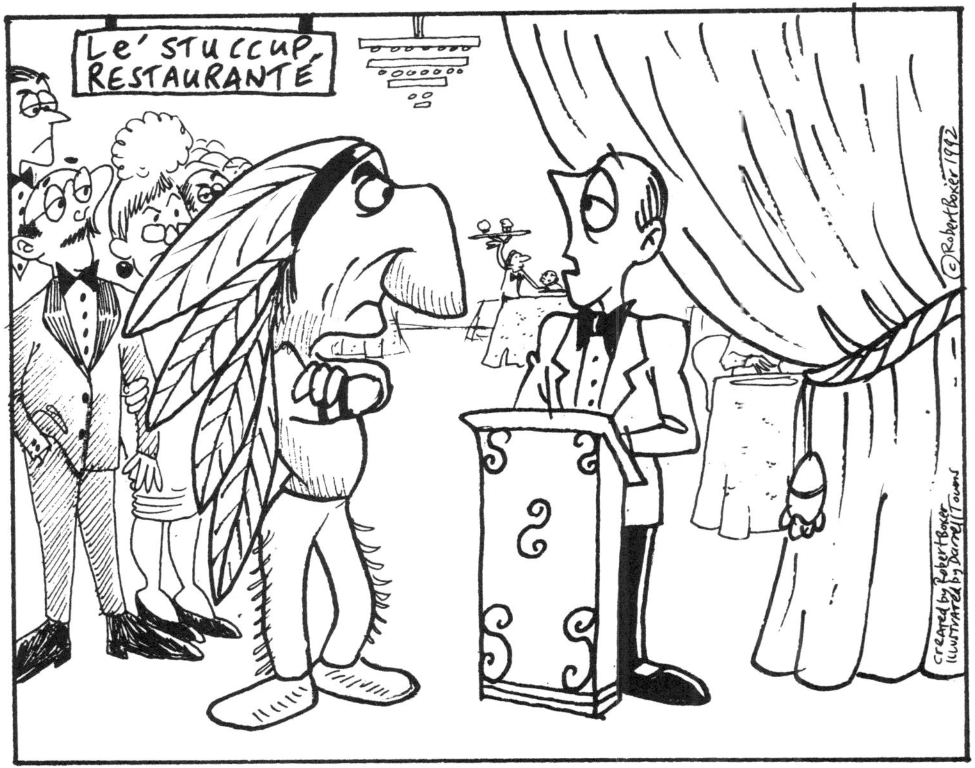
Le' STUCCUP
RESTAURANTÉ
©Robert Boxer 1992
created by Robert Boxer
Illustrated by Darrell Towns

"YOU SAY YOU DID HAVE A RESERVATION?"

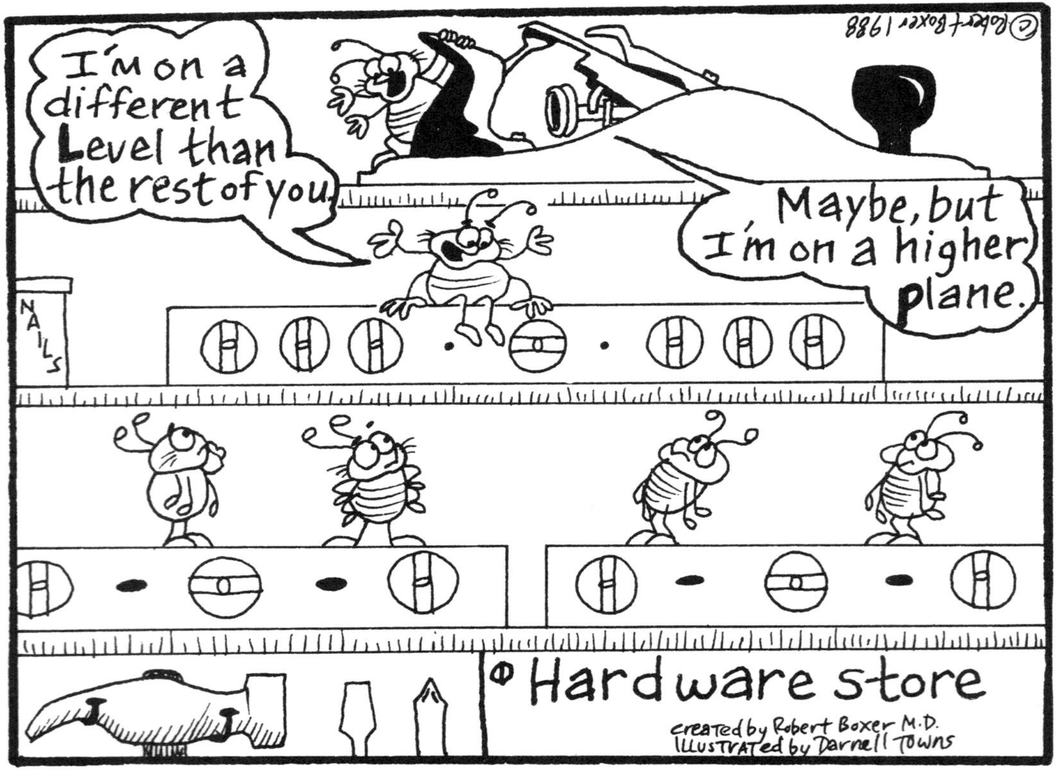

© Robert Boxer 1988
I'm on a different Level than the rest of you.
Maybe, but I'm on a higher plane.
NAILS
Hardware store
created by Robert Boxer M.D.
ILLUSTRATED by Darnell Towns

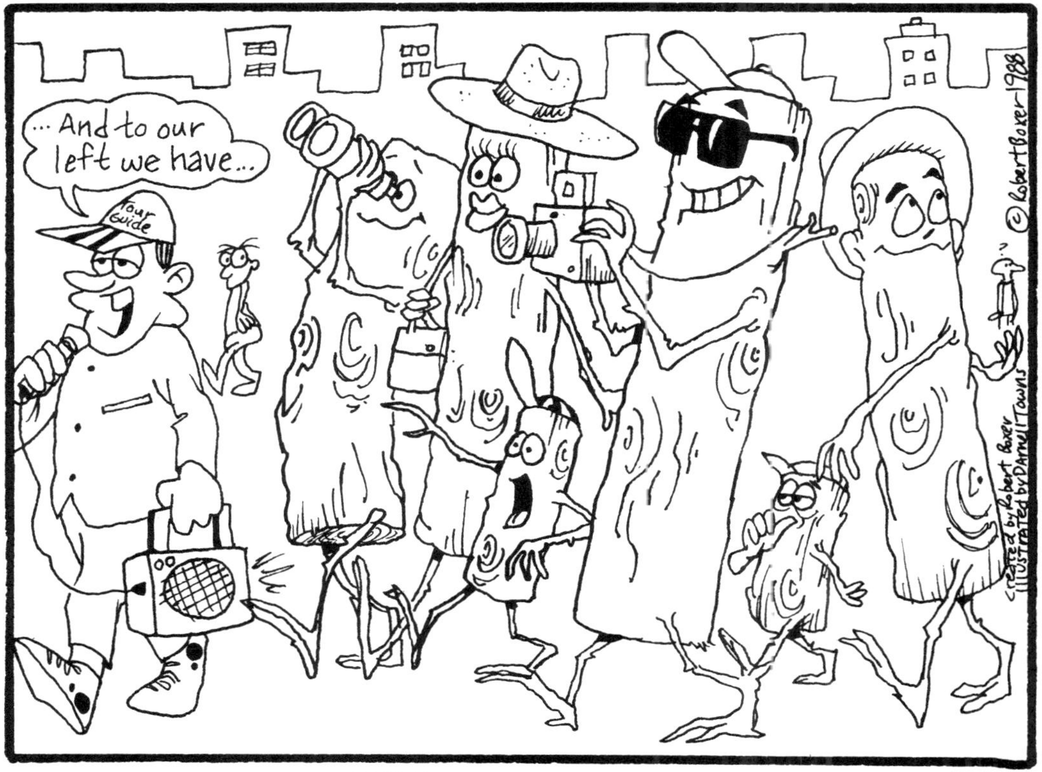
... And to our left we have...
Tour Guide
© Robert Boxer-1988
Created by Robert Boxer
Illustrated by Darnell Towns

TRAVEL LOGS

ANSWER DAT QUESTION
Number 2, What was the first movie that had to do with computers!
Good bye Mr. Chips!
1
2
3
3
692
280
Correct!
©Robert Boxer 1988
created by Robert Boxer M.D.
Illustrated by Darnell Towns

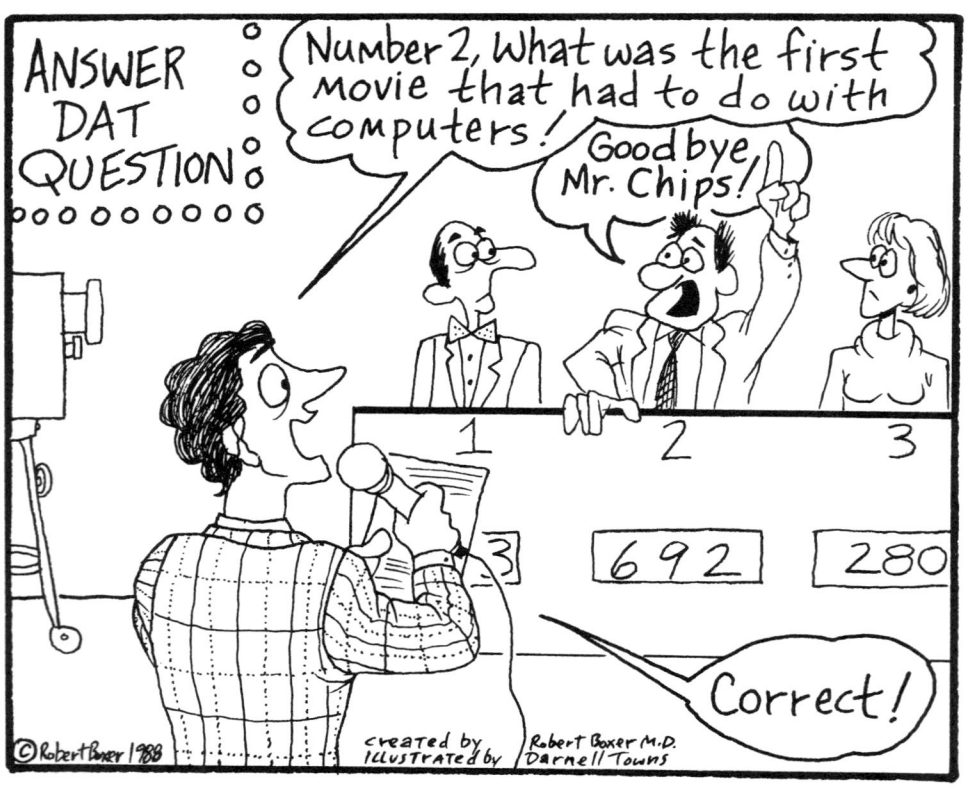

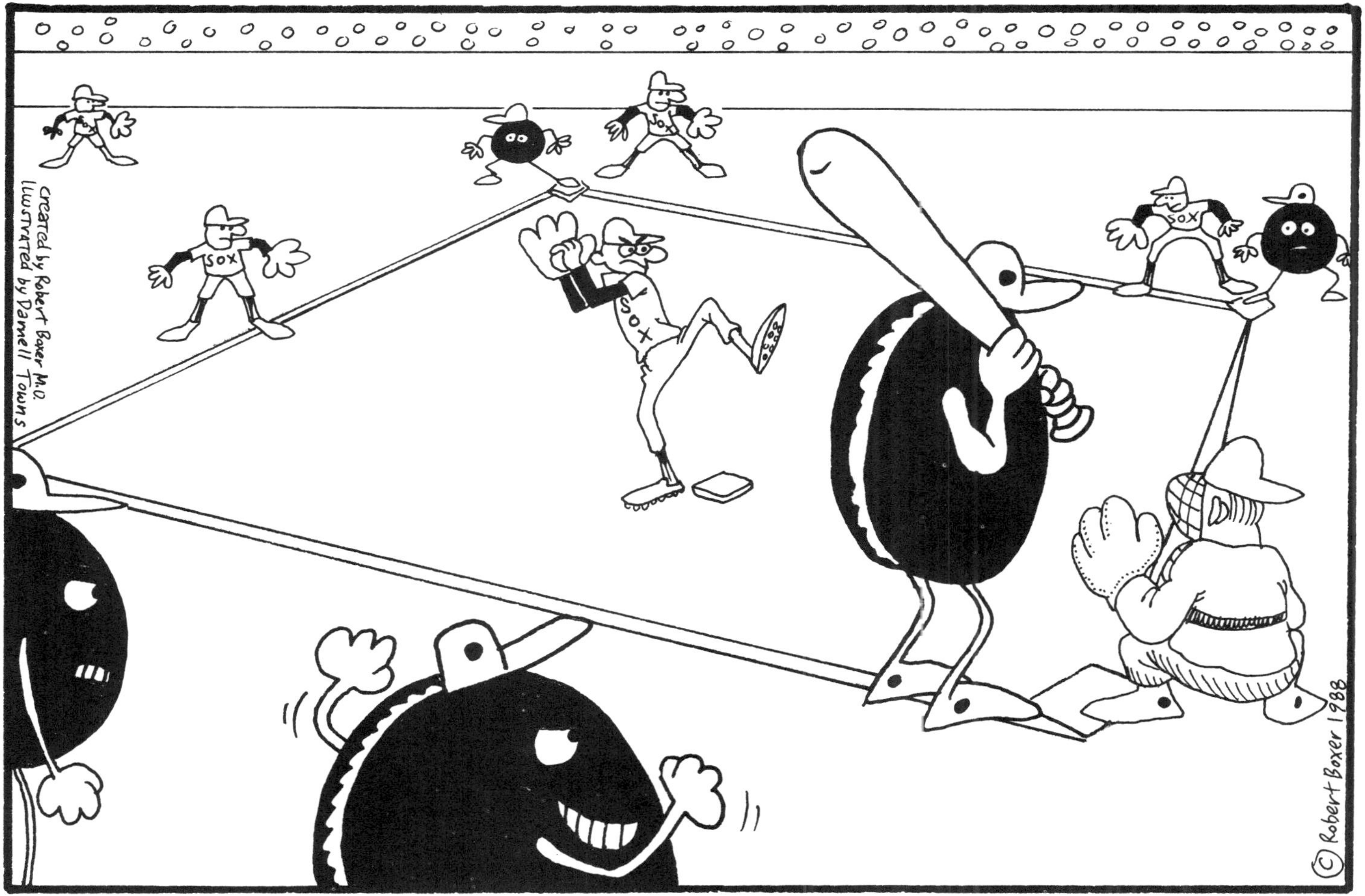
SOX
created by Robert Boxer M.D.
Illustrated by Darnell Towns
© Robert Boxer 1988

THE SOX PLAYING THE ORIOLES.

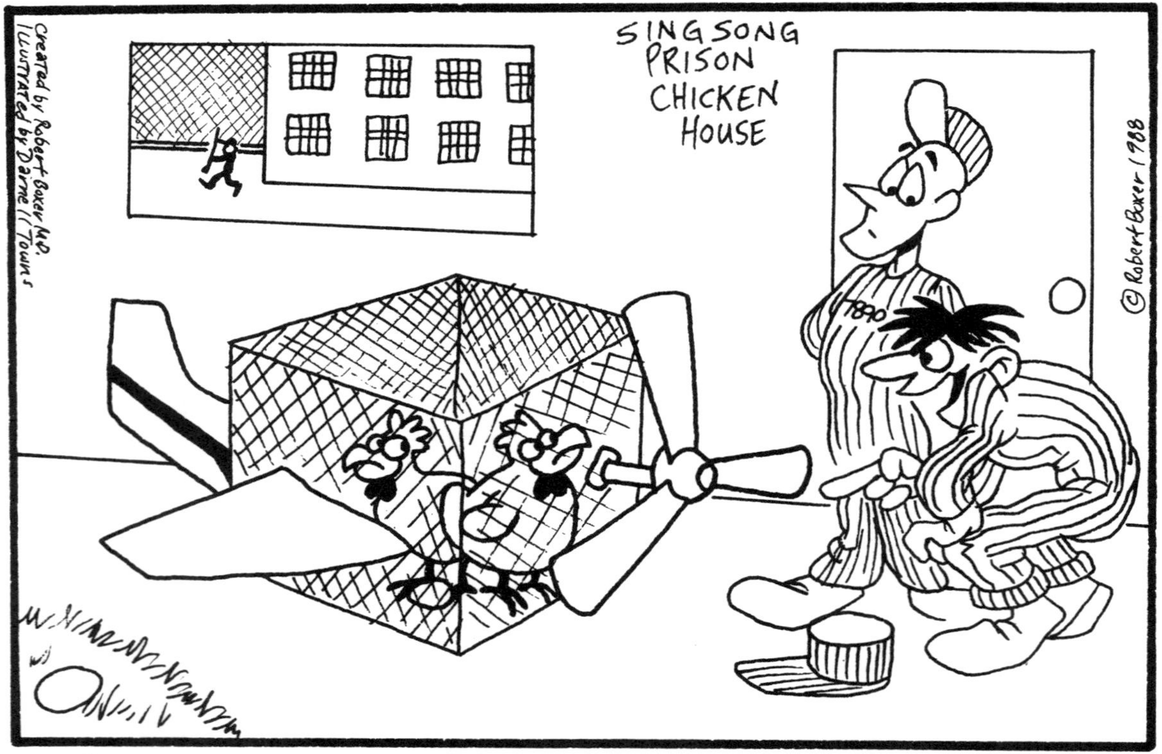
Created by Robert Boxer M.D.
Illustrated by Darnell Towns
SING SONG
PRISON
CHICKEN
HOUSE
7890
© Robert Boxer / 1988

"Tomorrow I'm plannin' to fly the Coop."

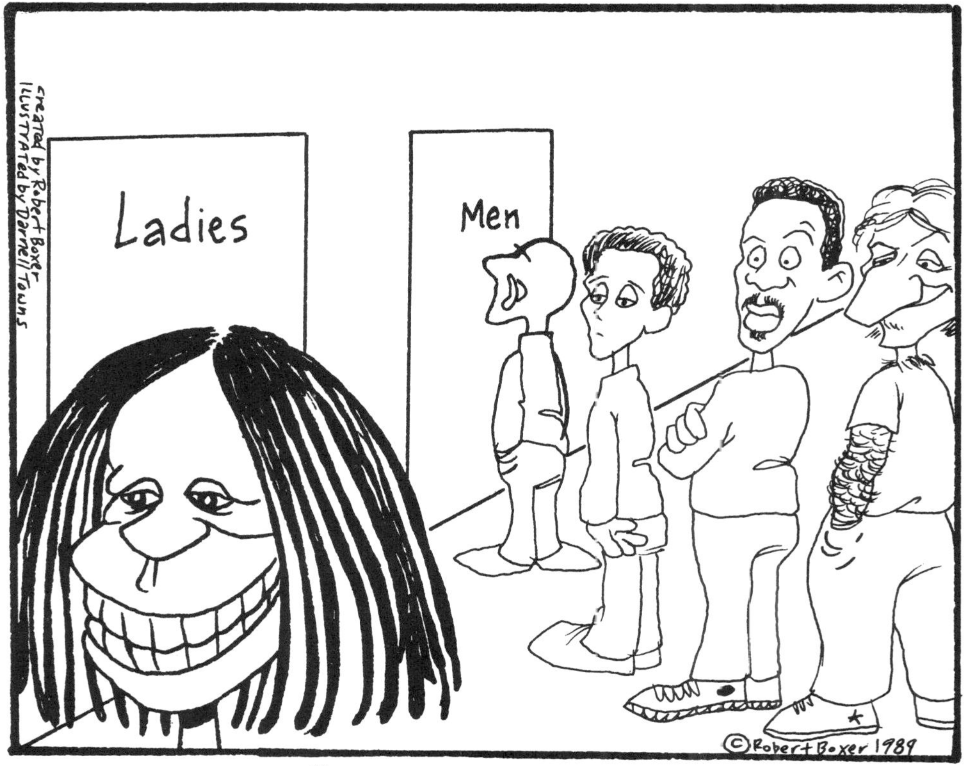
created by Robert Boxer
ILLUSTRATED by Darnell Towns
Ladies
Men
©Robert Boxer 1989

Comic Relief

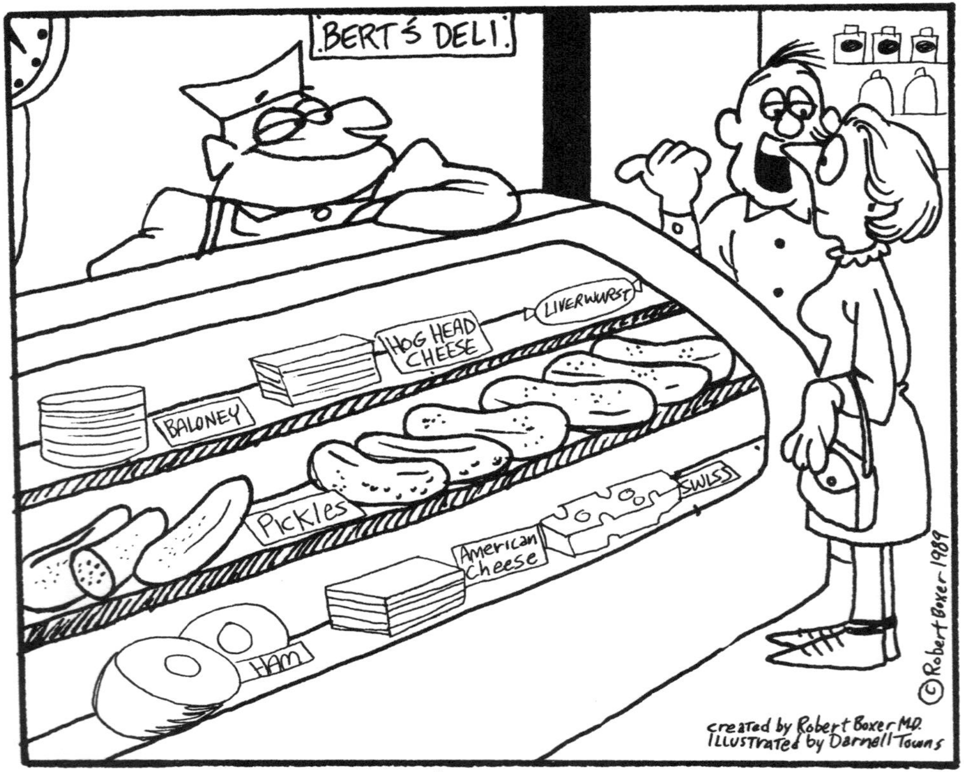
BERT'S DELI
LIVERWURST
HOG HEAD CHEESE
BALONEY
Pickles
SWISS
American Cheese
HAM
©Robert Boxer-1989
created by Robert Boxer M.D.
Illustrated by Darnell Towns

"If you're nice to this guy, maybe he'll cut you a **dill**."

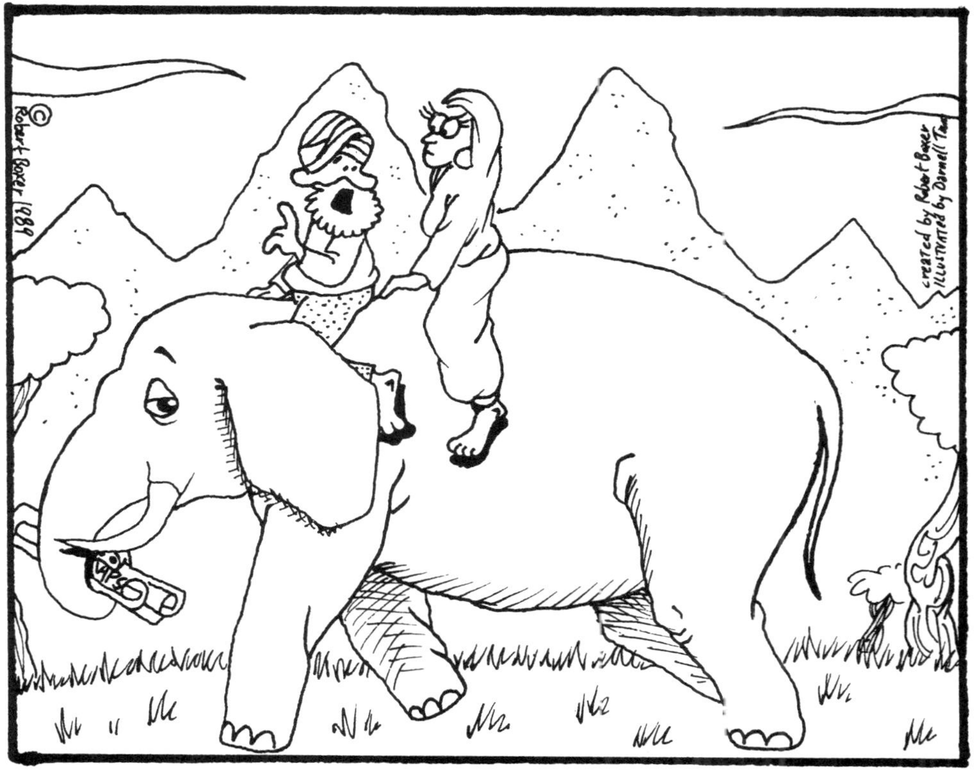
© Robert Boxer 1989
created by Robert Boxer

"At our next stop remind me to get the maps out of the trunk."

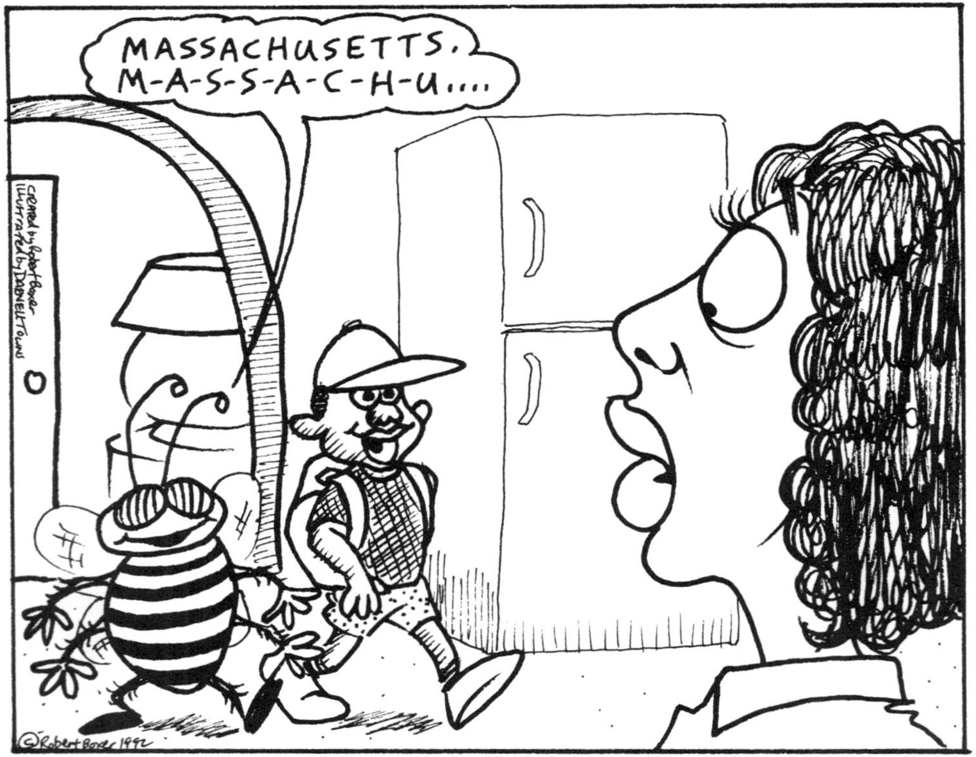
MASSACHUSETTS. M-A-S-S-A-C-H-U....
CREATED by Robert Boyer
ILLUSTRATED by DARNELL TOWNS
©Robert Boyer 1992

"Guess what, Mom,... I won the Spelling Bee today."

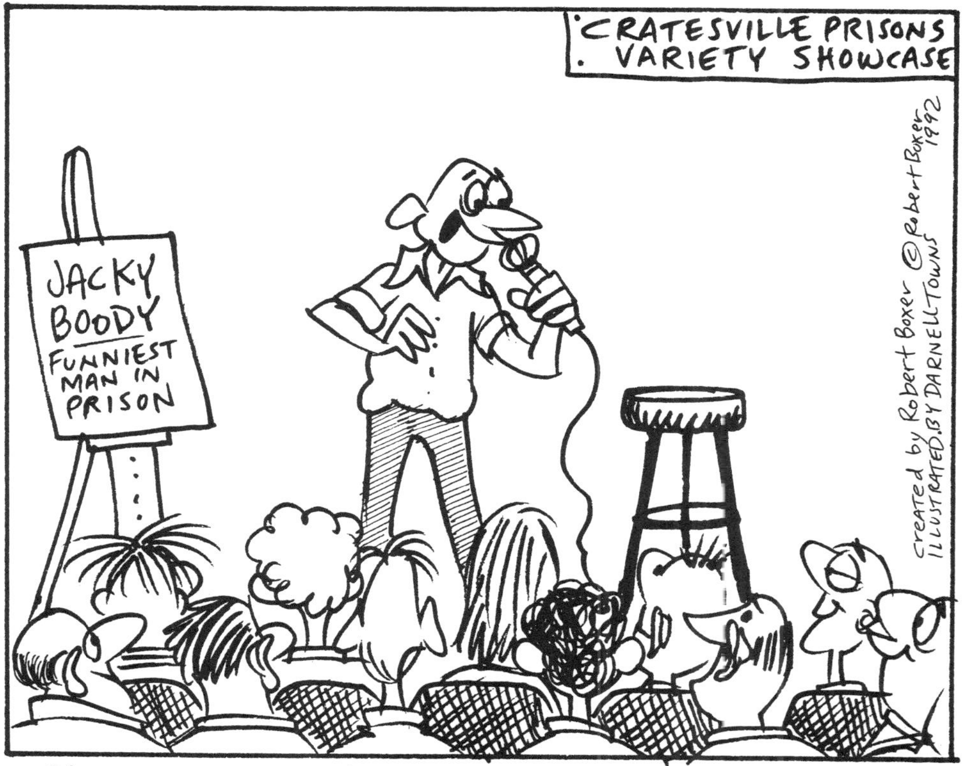
CRATESVILLE PRISONS
VARIETY SHOWCASE
JACKY BOODY
FUNNIEST MAN IN PRISON
Created by Robert Boxer © Robert Boxer 1992
ILLUSTRATED BY DARNELL TOWNS

"Please, don't interrupt me in the middle of a SENTENCE."

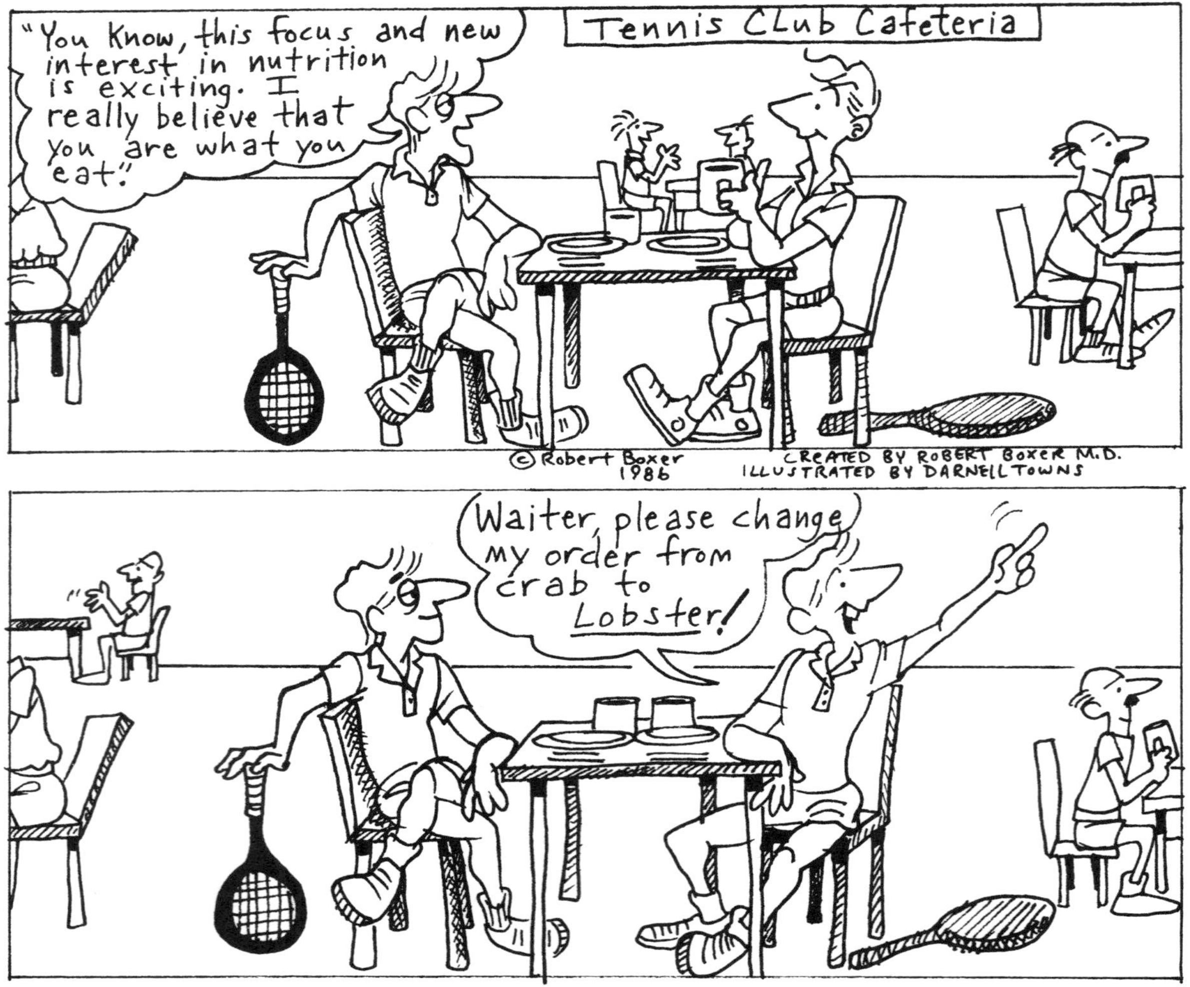
Tennis Club Cafeteria
"You know, this focus and new interest in nutrition is exciting. I really believe that you are what you eat."
© Robert Boxer 1986
CREATED BY ROBERT BOXER M.D.
ILLUSTRATED BY DARNELL TOWNS
Waiter, please change my order from crab to Lobster!

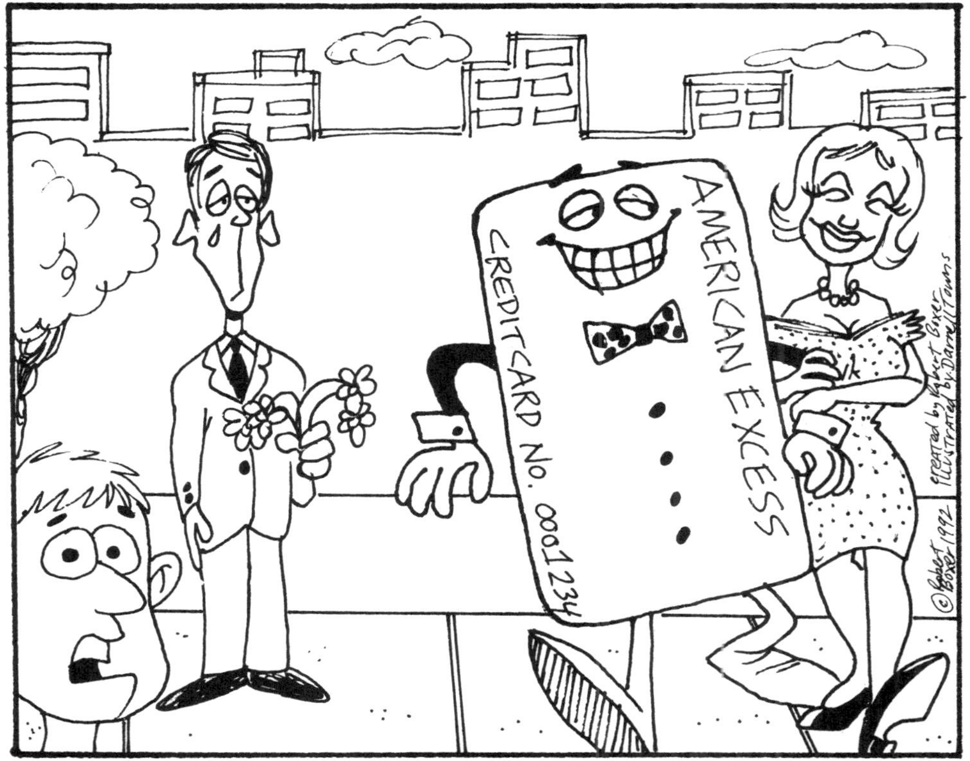
AMERICAN EXCESS
CREDIT CARD No. 0001234

"Well....he did tell me that he **had been** turned down for a Credit Card."

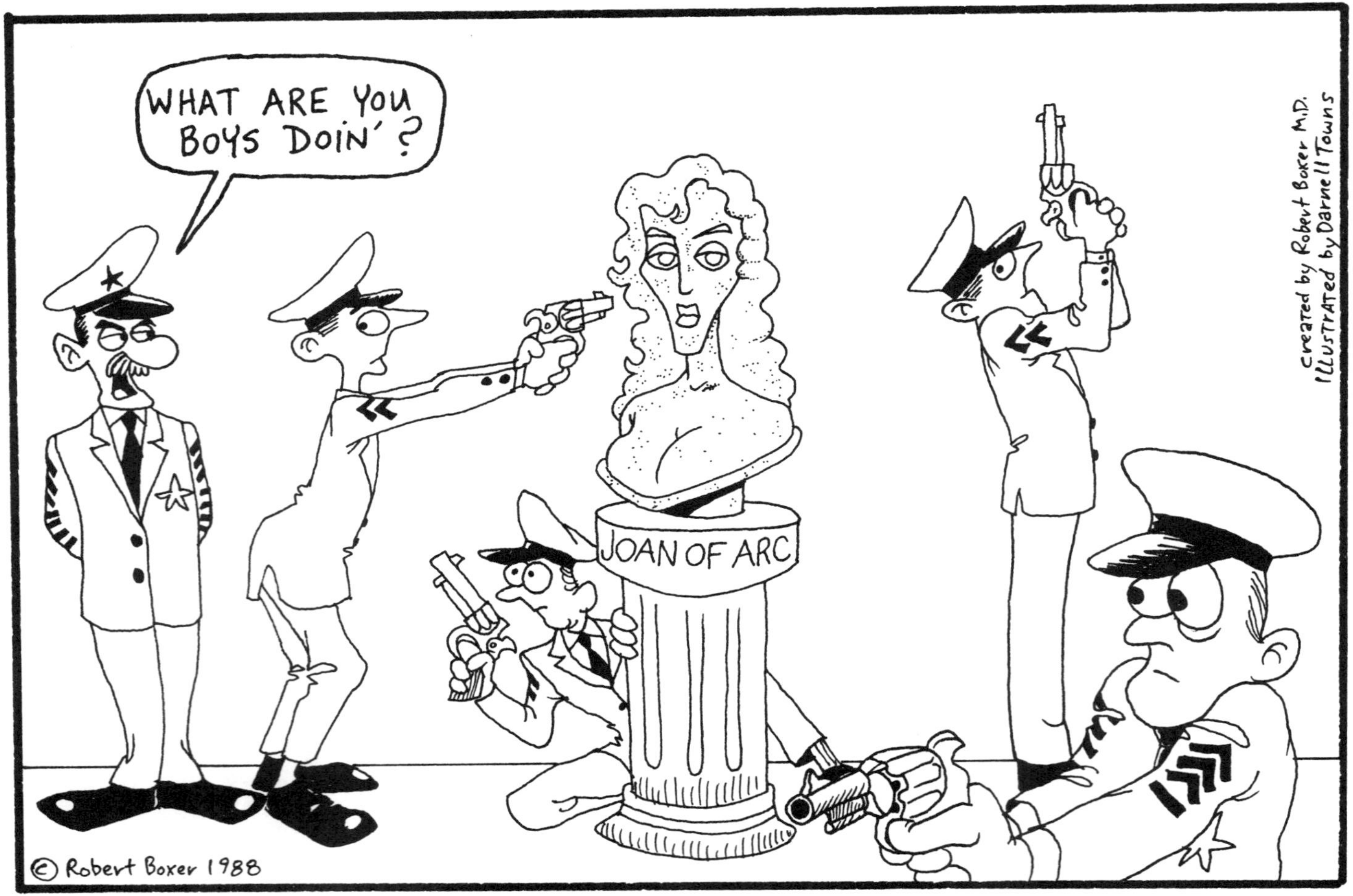
WHAT ARE YOU BOYS DOIN'?
JOAN OF ARC
Created by Robert Boxer M.D.
Illustrated by Darnell Towns
© Robert Boxer 1988

HEROINE BUST

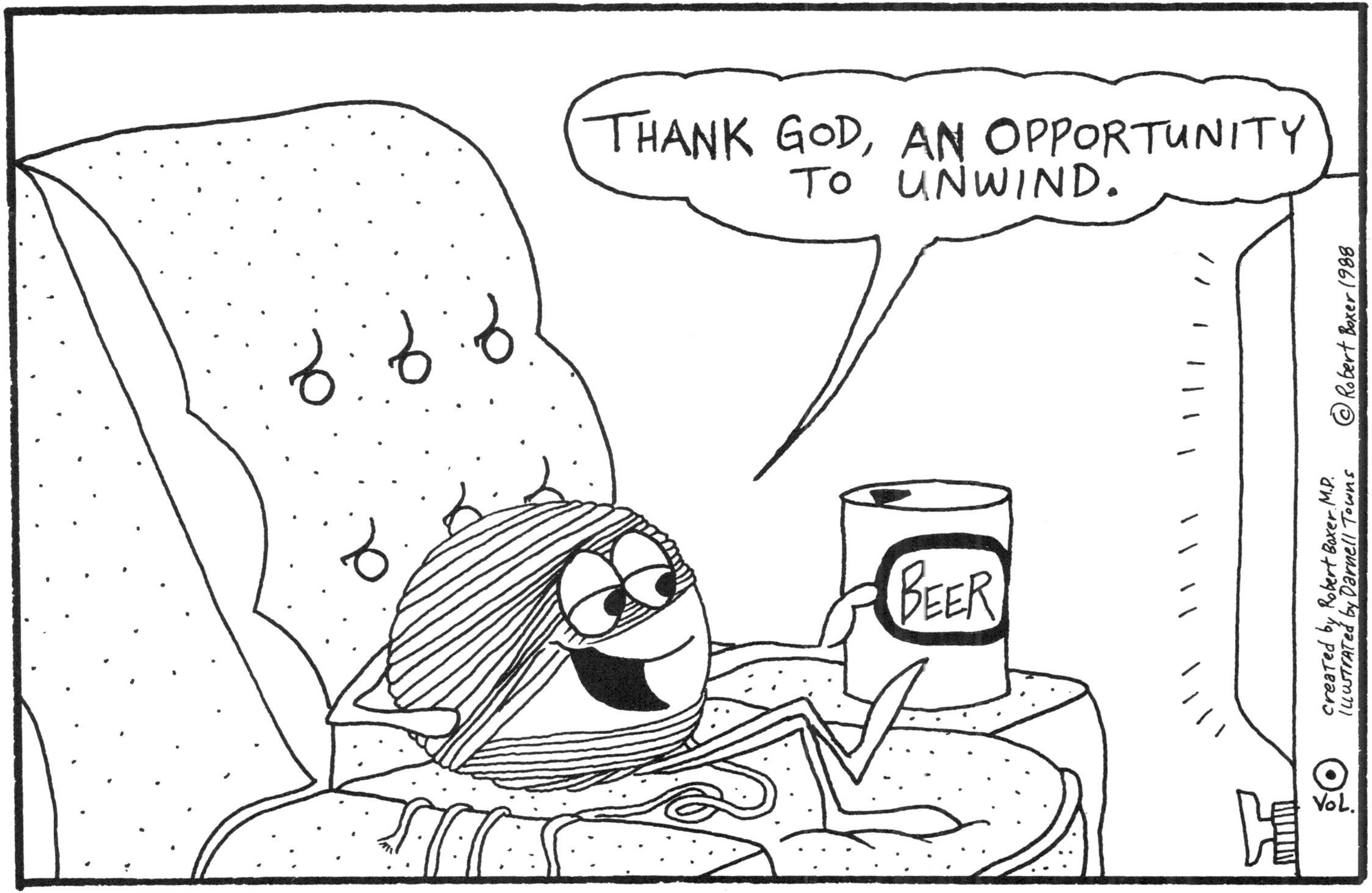
THANK GOD, AN OPPORTUNITY TO UNWIND.
BEER
VOL.
created by Robert Boxer M.D.
ILLUSTRATED by Darnell Towns
© Robert Boxer 1988

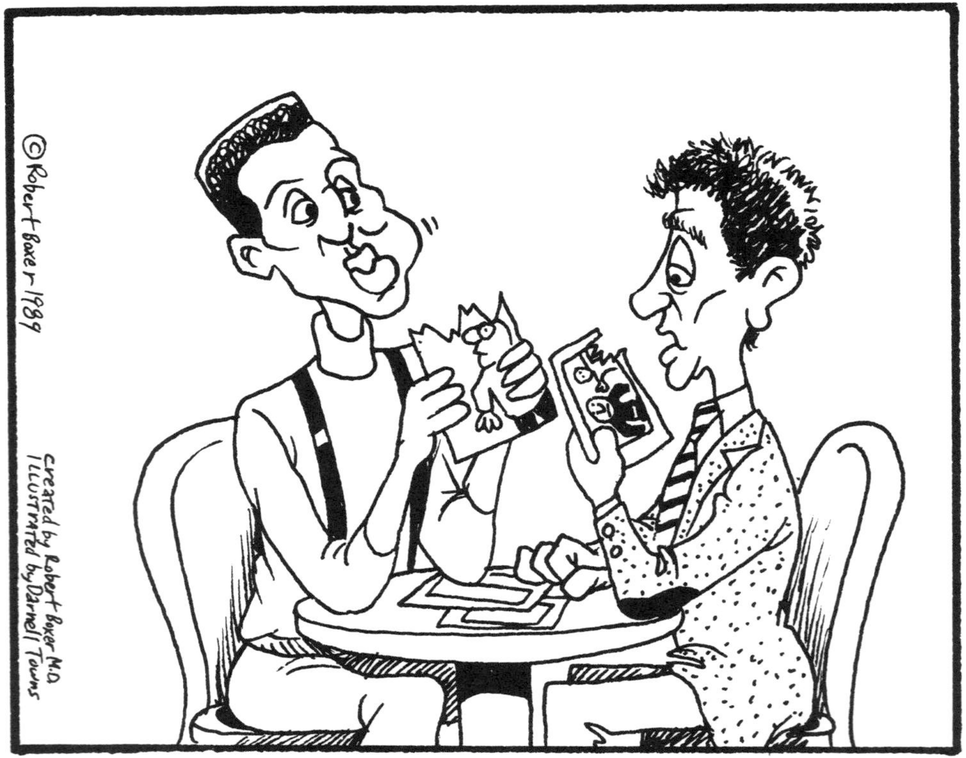
©Robert Baker 1989
created by Robert Baker M.D.
Illustrated by Darnell Towns

"You're right, Darnell, these cartoons are tasteless."

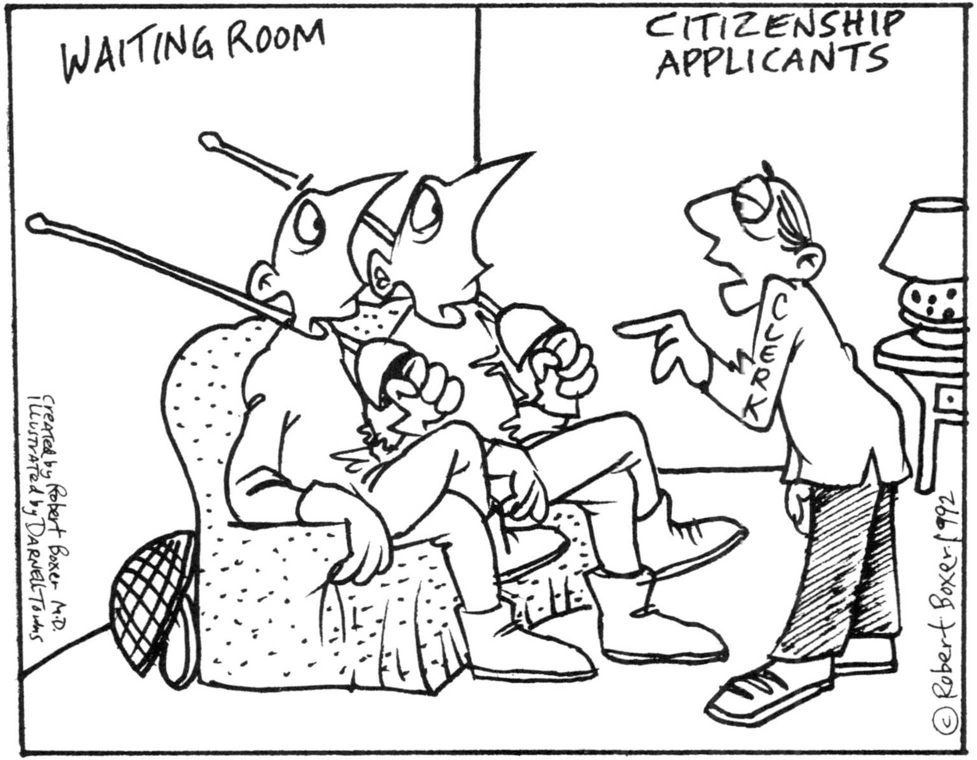
WAITING ROOM
CITIZENSHIP APPLICANTS
CLERK
CREATED by Robert Boxer M.D.
ILLUSTRATED by DARNELL TOWNS
© Robert Boxer 1992

"Are you two applying for DUAL citizenship?"

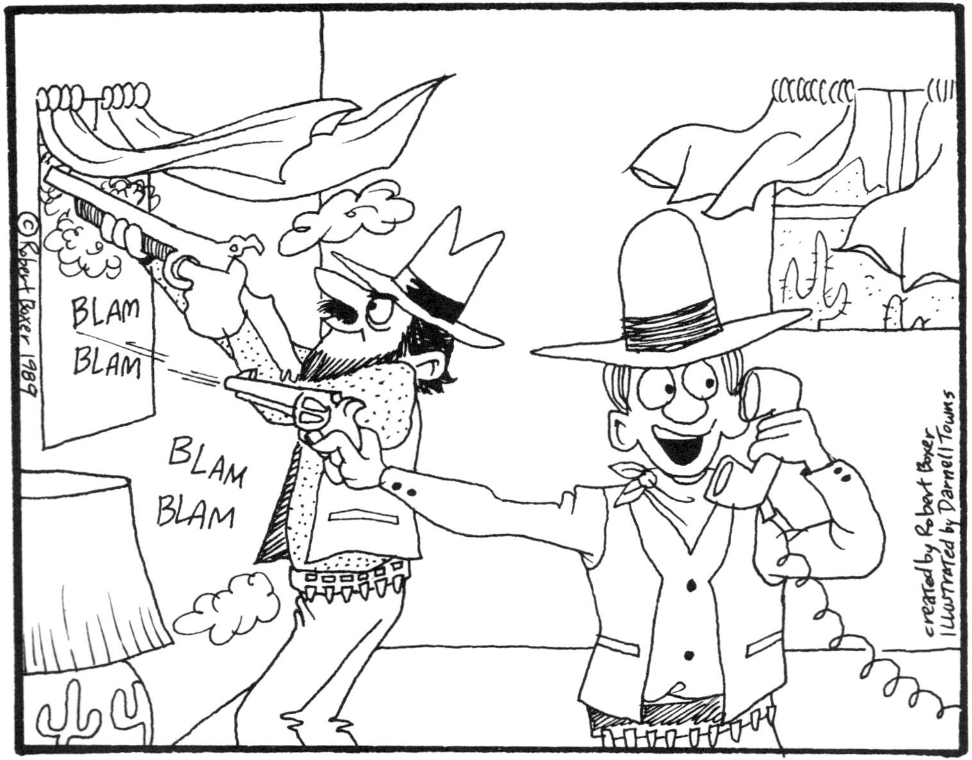
BLAM
BLAM
BLAM
BLAM
© Robert Boxer 1989
created by Robert Boxer
ILLUSTRATED by Darnell Towns

"Yeah, me and my dad are just shooting the breeze."

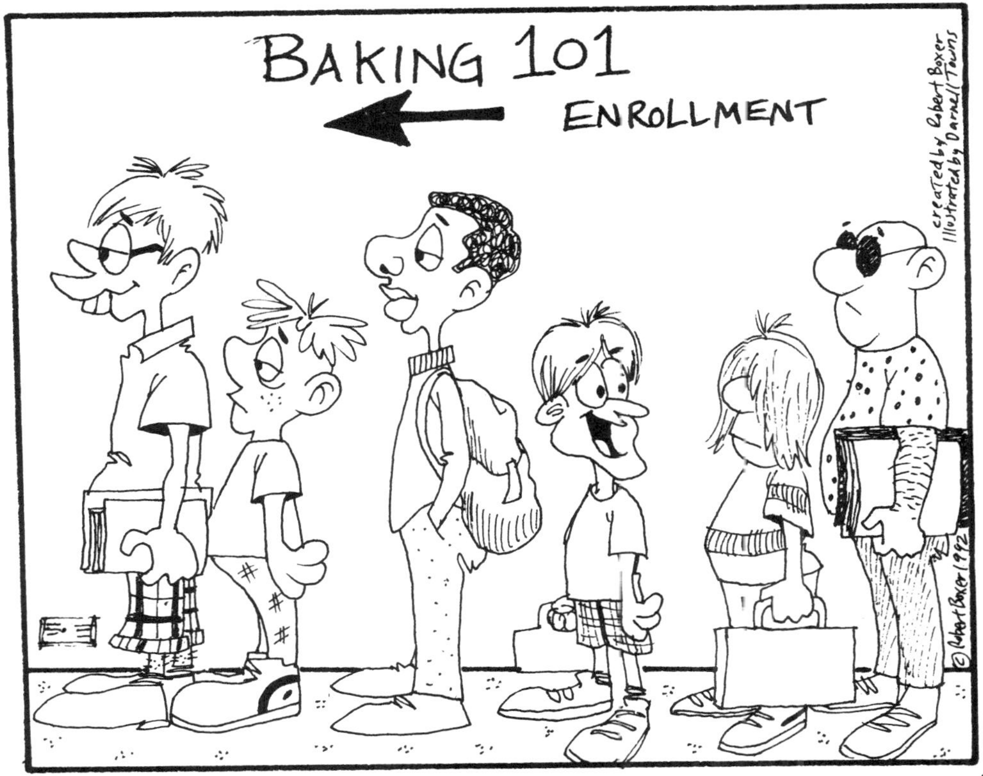
BAKING 101
ENROLLMENT
created by Robert Boxer
Illustrated by Darnell Towns
© Robert Boxer 1992

"I HEARD THIS COURSE WAS A PIECE OF CAKE."

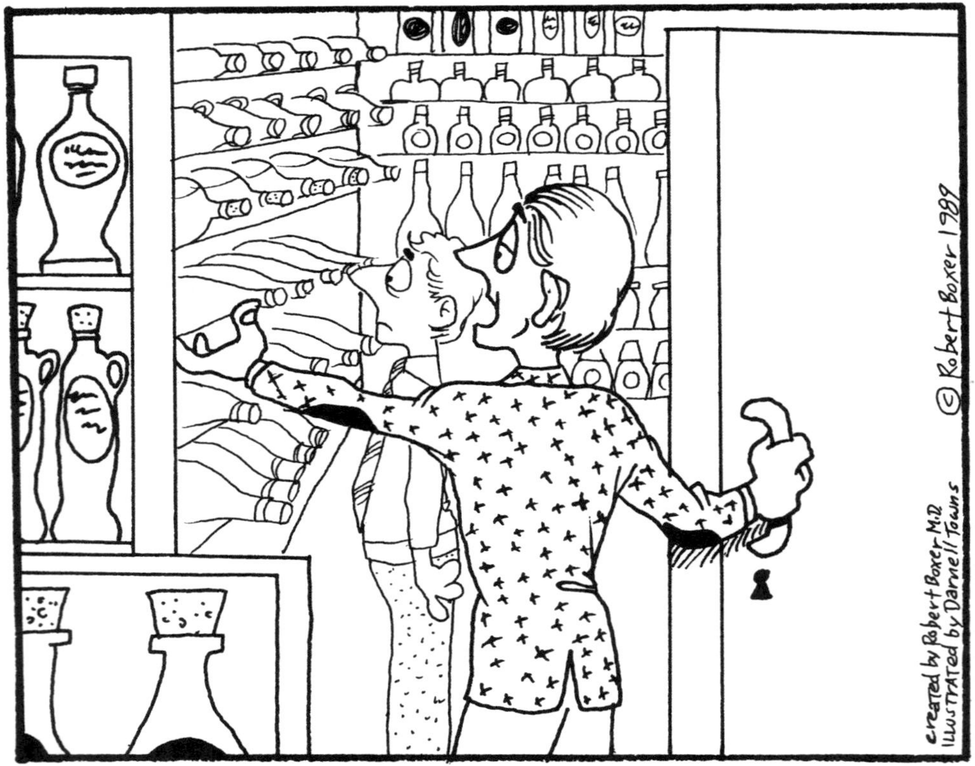
© Robert Boxer 1989
created by Robert Boxer M.D.
ILLUSTRATED by Darnell Towns

"This is on everyone's best Cellar list."

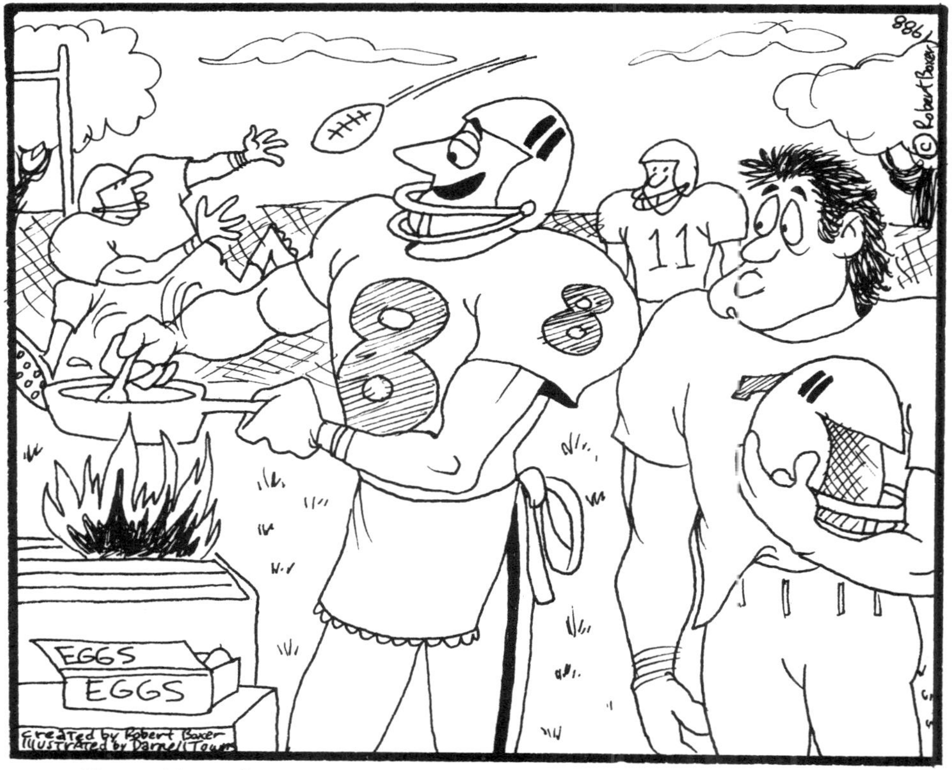

© Robert Baxer 1988
11
88
EGGS
EGGS
Created by Robert Baxer
Illustrated by Darrell Towns

"Well, the coach said I had to master the Art of Scrambling."

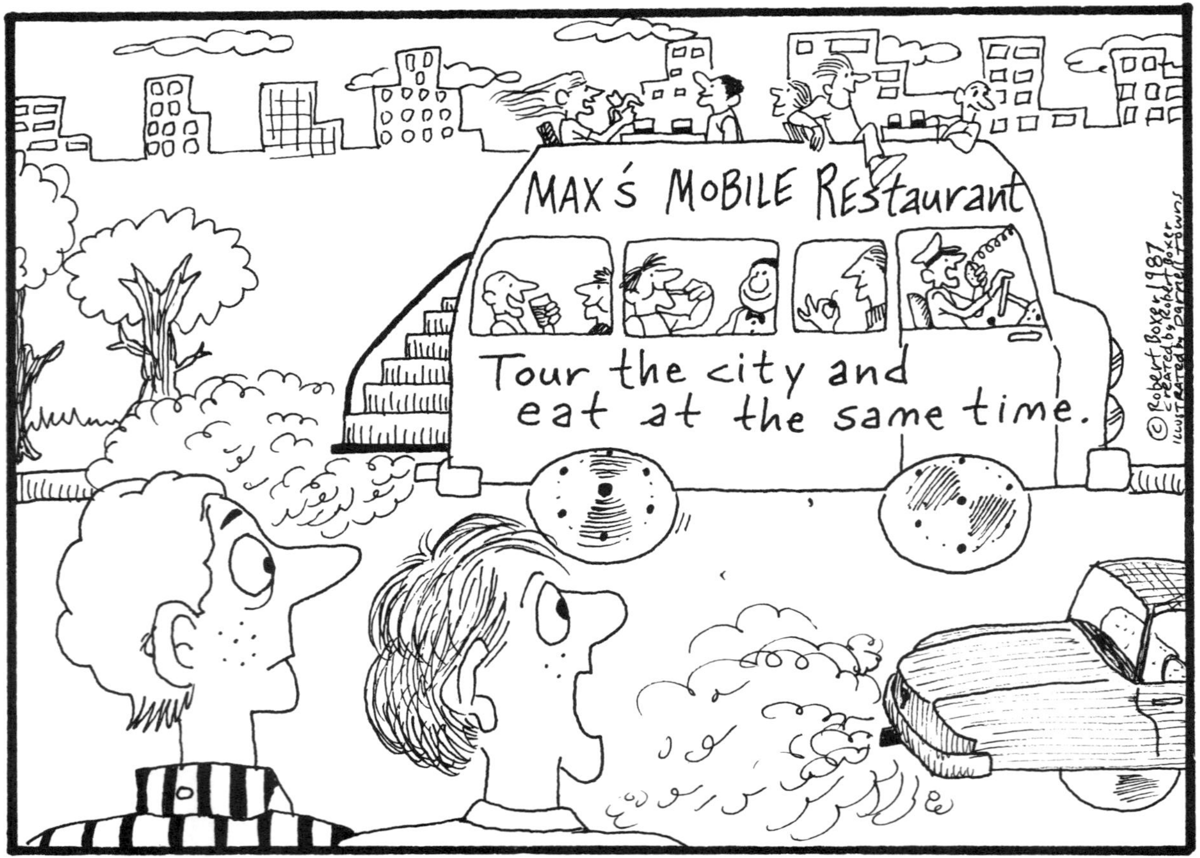
MAX'S MOBILE RESTAURANT
Tour the city and eat at the same time.
© Robert Boxer 1987
CREATED by Robert Boxer
ILLUSTRATED by Darnell Towns

"THAT'S WHERE I LEARNED TO BE A BUS BOY."

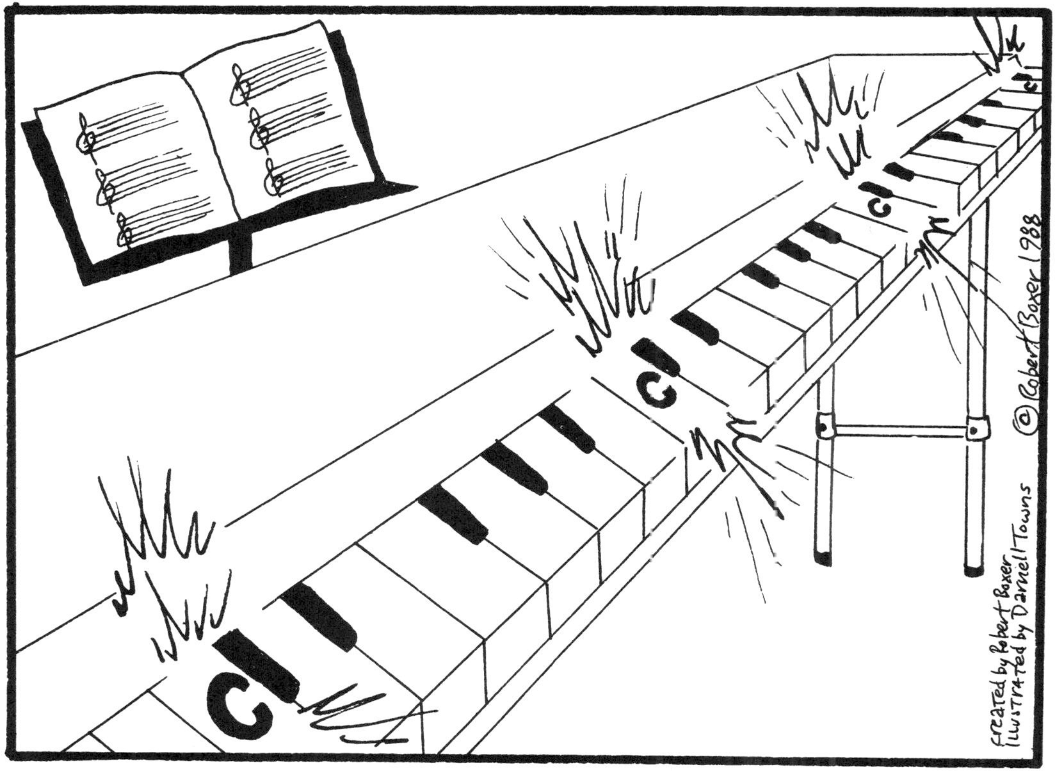
© Robert Boxer 1988
created by Robert Boxer
illustrated by Daniel Towns

FROM SEA TO SHINING SEA.

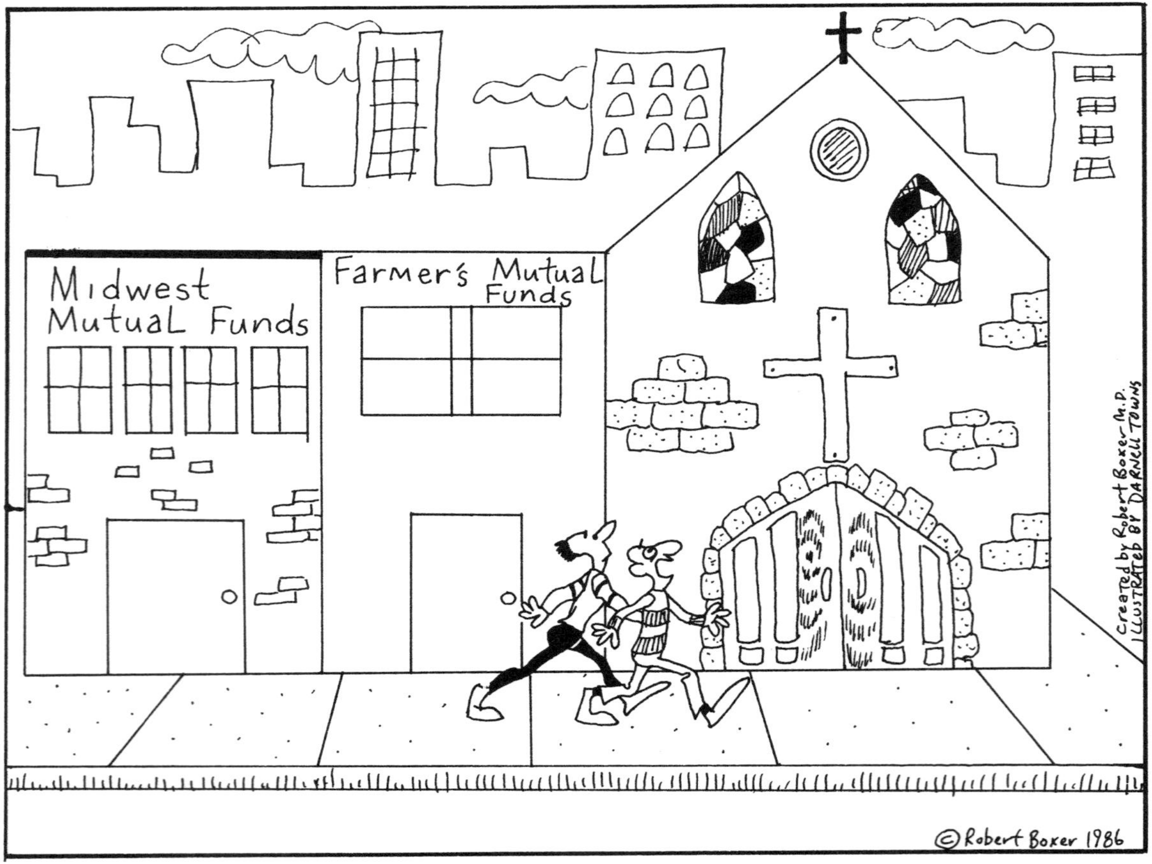
Midwest
Mutual Funds
Farmer's Mutual
Funds
Created by Robert Boxer M.D.
ILLUSTRATED BY DARNELL TOWNS
©Robert Boxer 1986

"I hear there are no dues, but there is a one percent redemption fee".

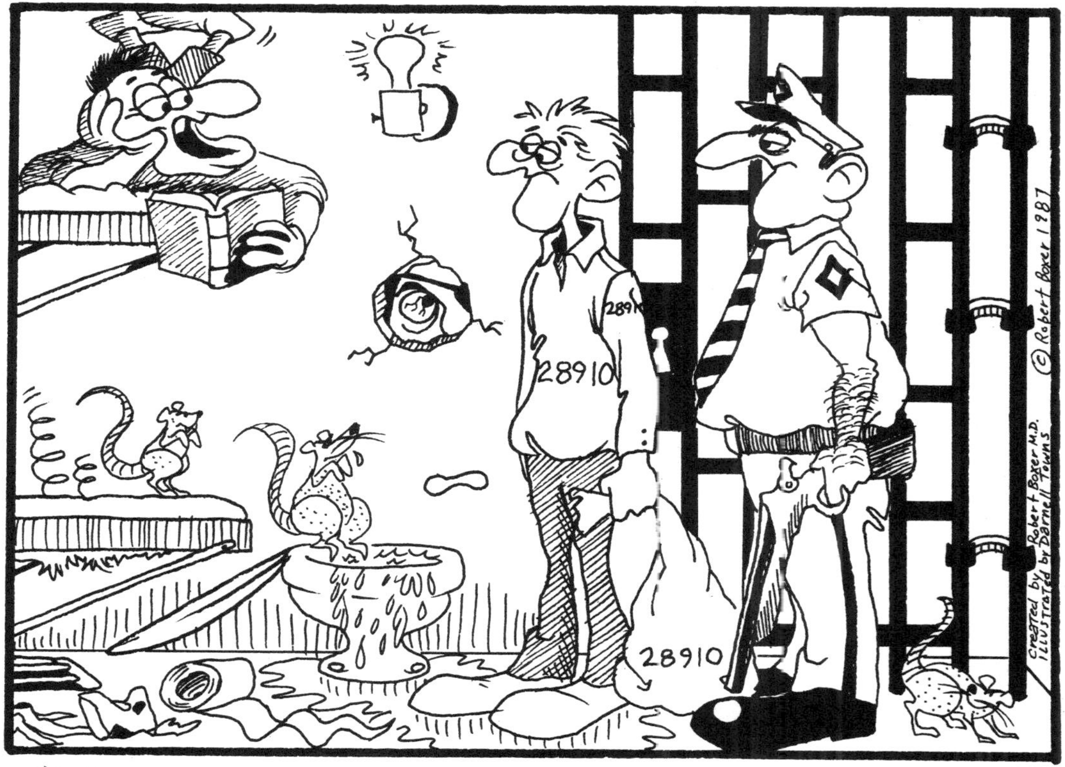
28910
28910
© Robert Boxer 1987
Created by Robert Boxer M.D.
Illustrated by Darnell Towns

"What did you expect, the 'Cell of the Century?"

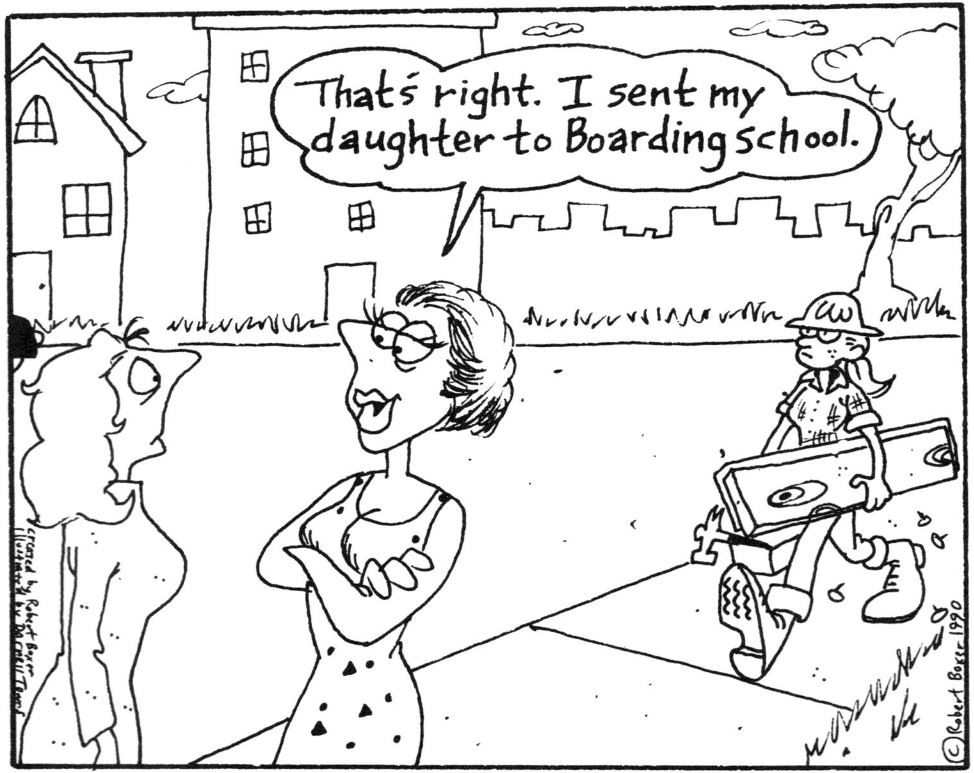
That's right. I sent my daughter to Boarding school.

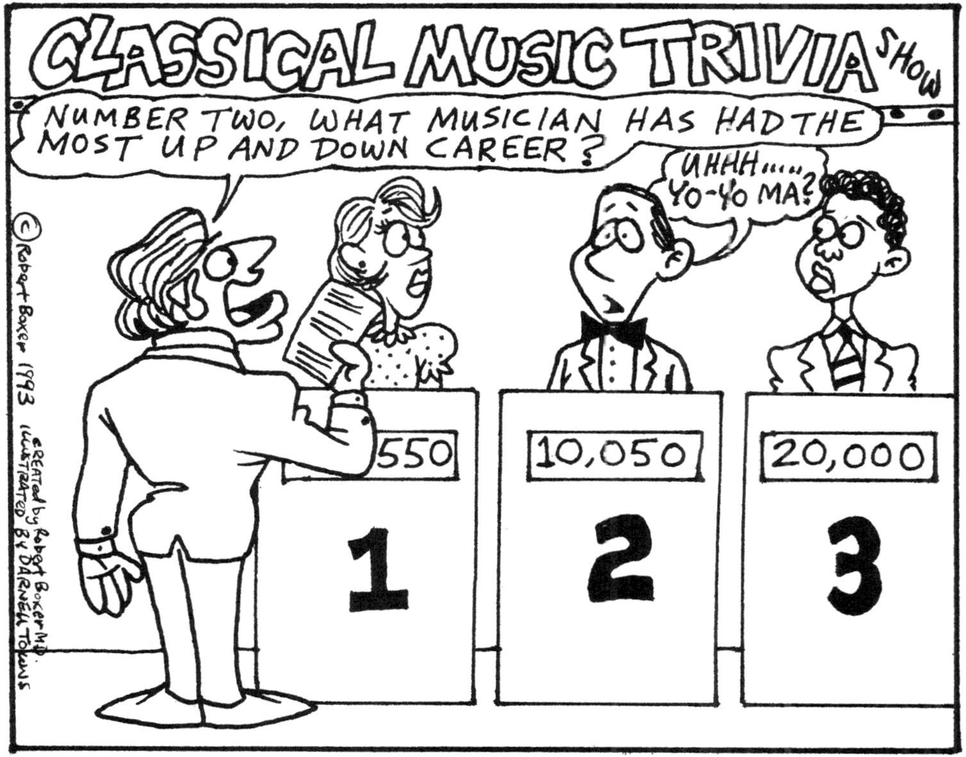
CLASSICAL MUSIC TRIVIA SHOW
NUMBER TWO, WHAT MUSICIAN HAS HAD THE MOST UP AND DOWN CAREER?
UHHH..... YO-YO MA?
550
10,050
20,000
1
2
3
© Robert Boxer 1993
CREATED by Robert Boxer M.D.
ILLUSTRATED BY DARNELL TOWNS

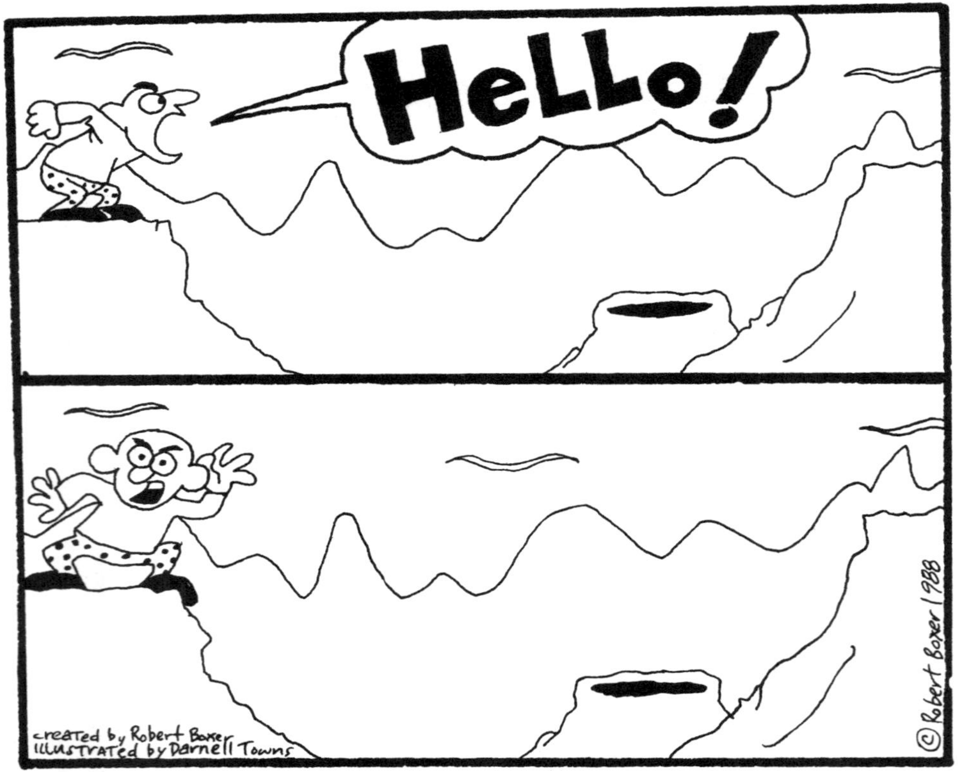
HELLO!
created by Robert Boxer
illustrated by Darnell Towns
© Robert Boxer 1988

"I think all our pollution has permanently damaged our ECHO SYSTEM."

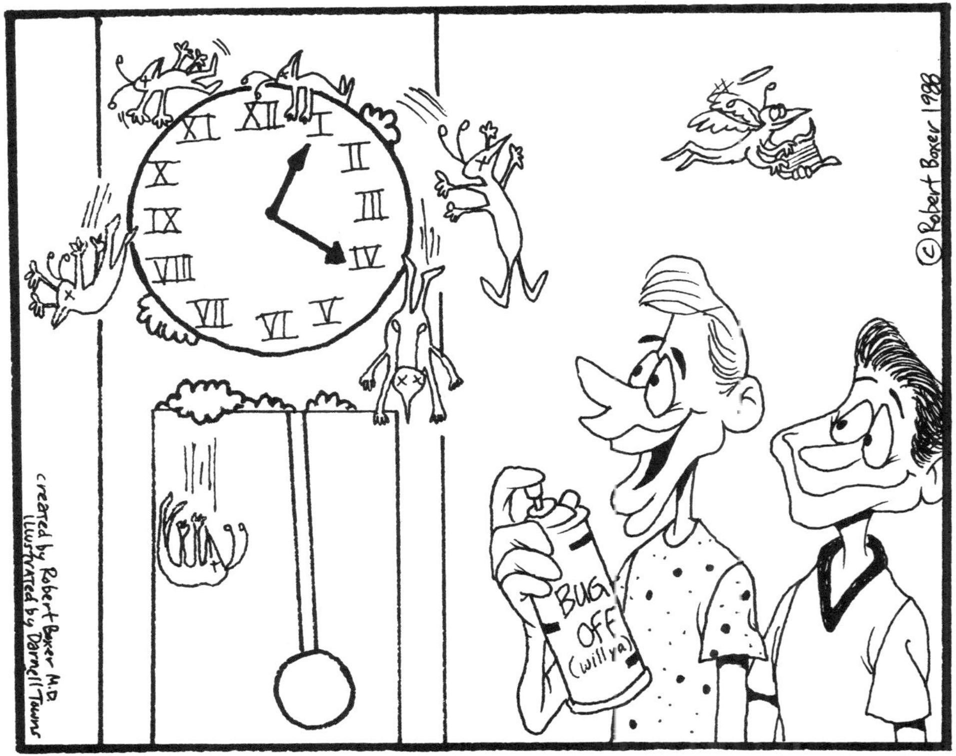
BUG OFF (willya)
© Robert Boxer 1988
created by Robert Boxer M.D.
illustrated by Darnell Towns

"I told you this stuff was guaranteed to kill roaches AROUND THE CLOCK."

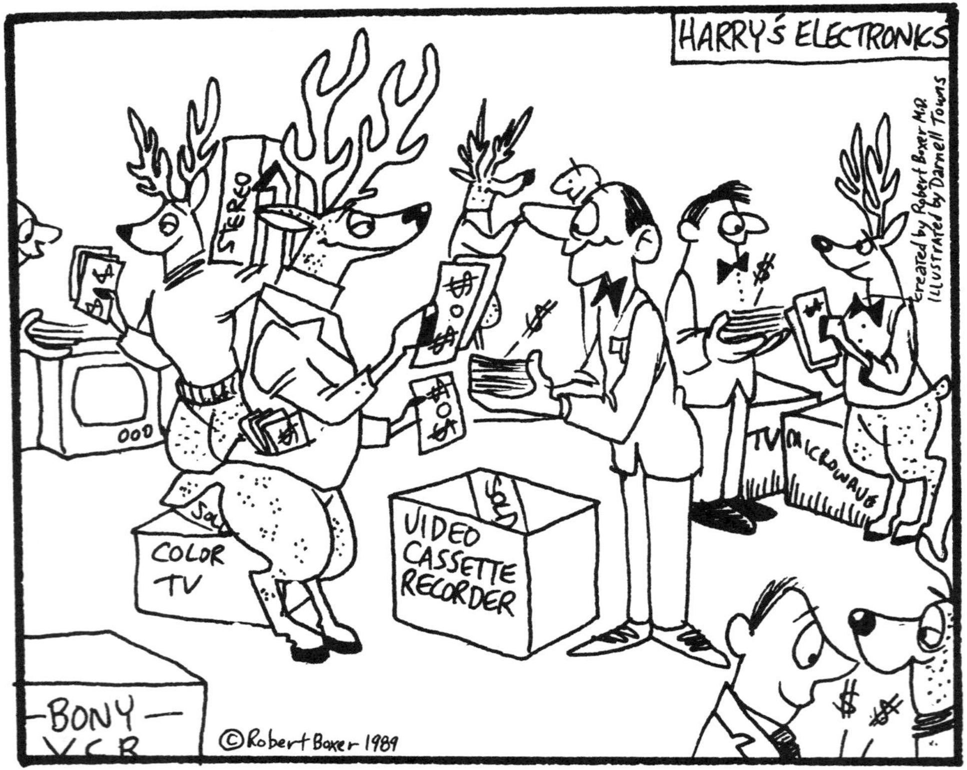
HARRY'S ELECTRONICS
Created by Robert Boxer M.D.
Illustrated by Darnell Towns
STEREO
COLOR TV
VIDEO CASSETTE RECORDER
TV
MICROWAVE
BONY
©Robert Boxer 1989

Big **B**uck Spending.

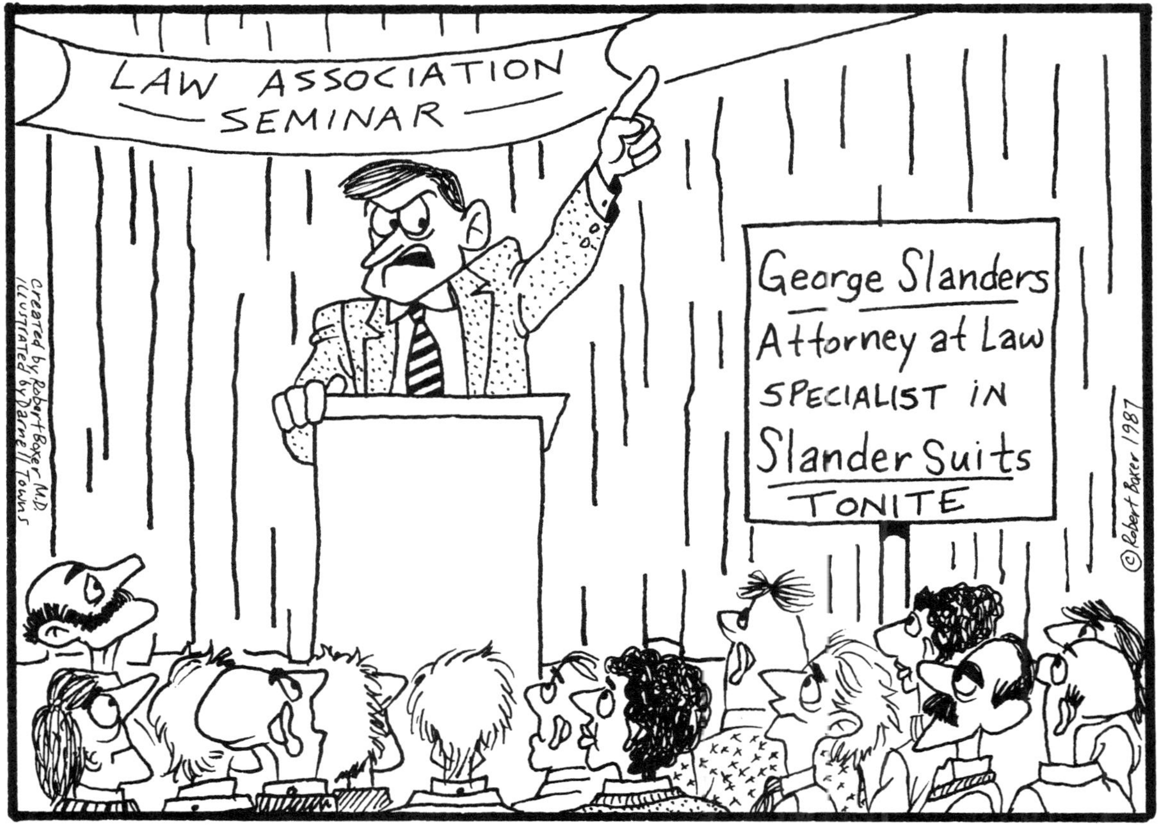
LAW ASSOCIATION
SEMINAR
George Slanders
Attorney at Law
SPECIALIST IN
Slander Suits
TONITE
Created by Robert Baker M.D.
Illustrated by Darnell Towns
© Robert Baker 1987

"You **can** judge a **suit** by its **libel**."

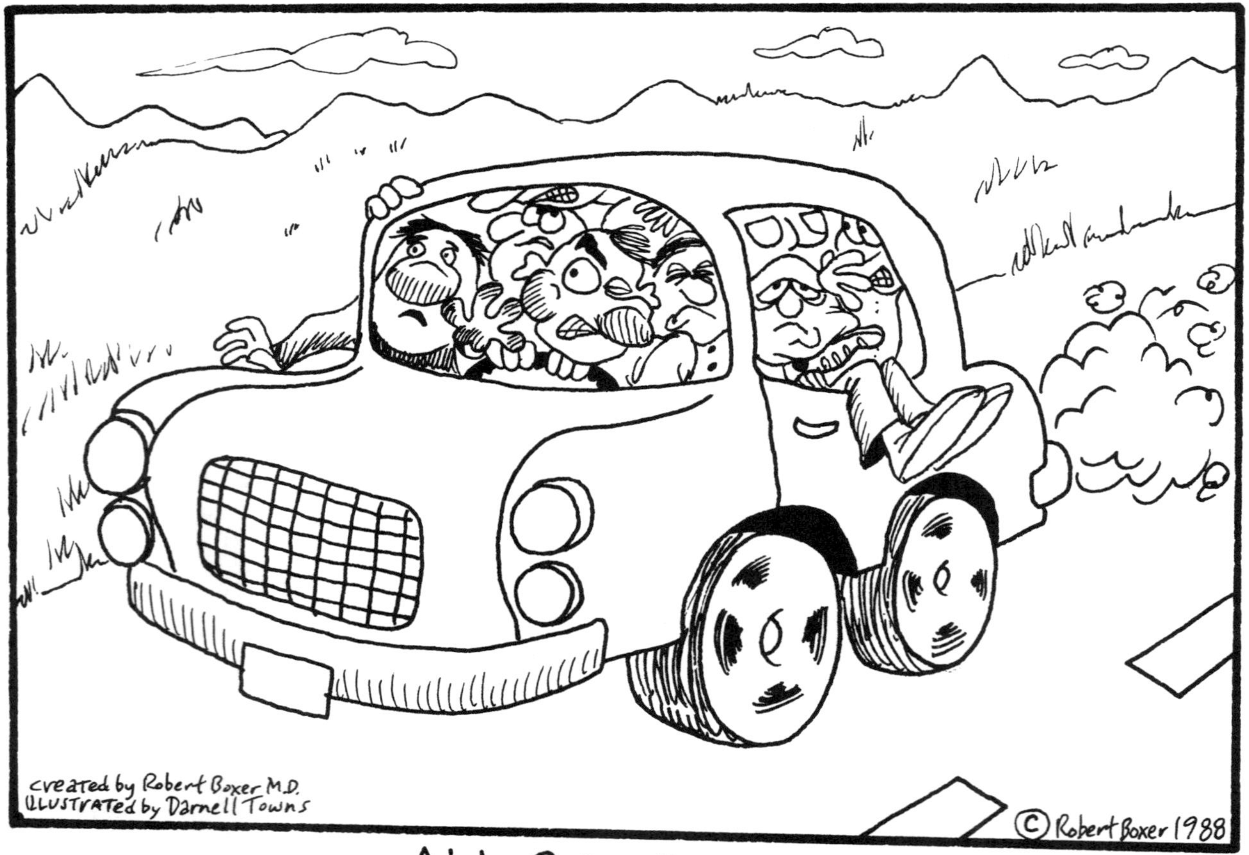
created by Robert Boxer M.D.
ILLUSTRATED by Darnell Towns
© Robert Boxer 1988

ALL COUPED UP

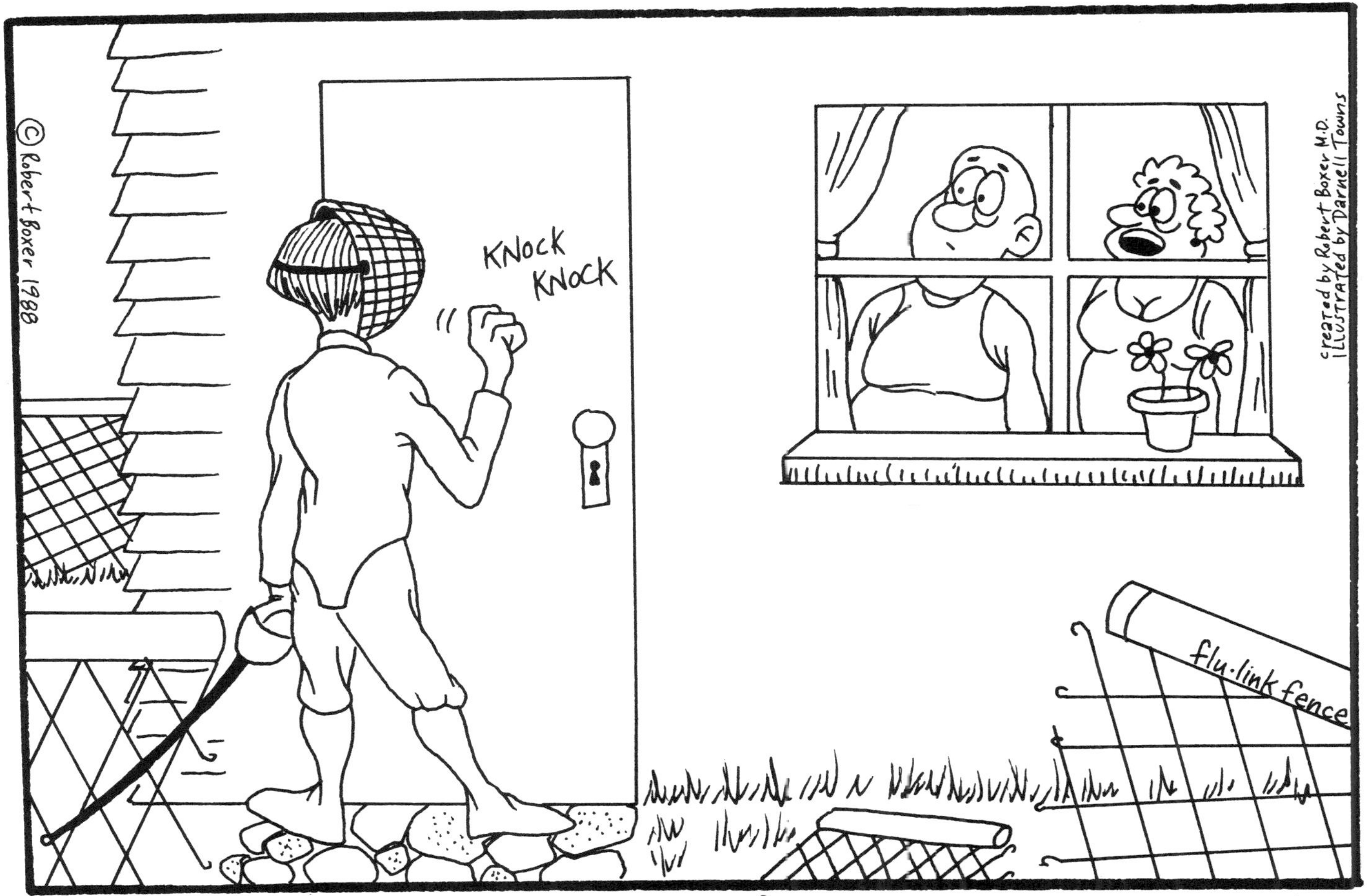
© Robert Boxer 1988
KNOCK KNOCK
created by Robert Boxer M.D.
Illustrated by Darnell Towns
flu·link fence

"You did tell me to call a fencer, didn't you?"

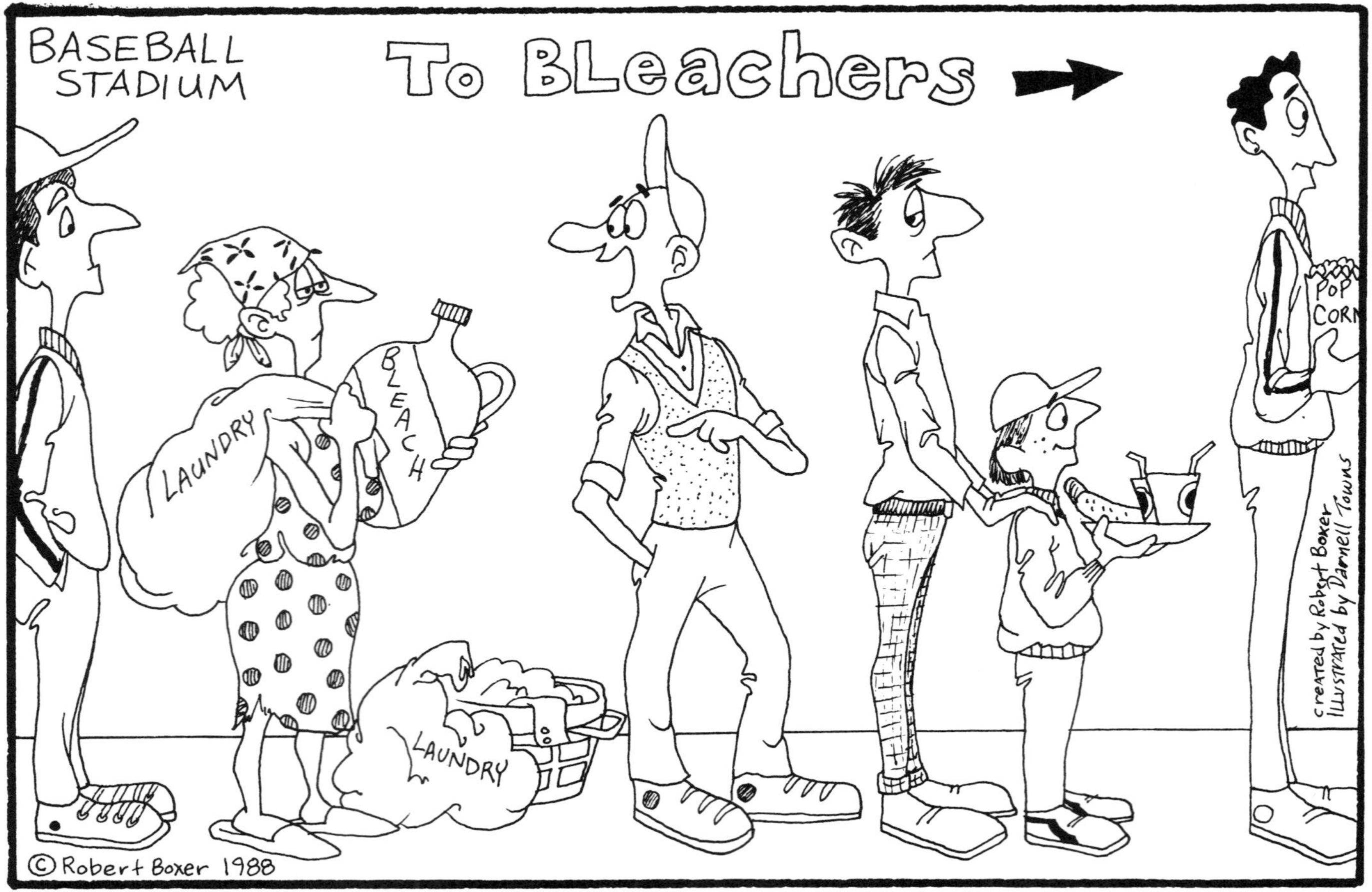
BASEBALL STADIUM
To BLeachers
LAUNDRY
BLEACH
LAUNDRY
POP CORN
created by Robert Boxer
ILLUSTRATED by Darnell Towns
© Robert Boxer 1988

"Hazel, I think you've got to learn more about sports".

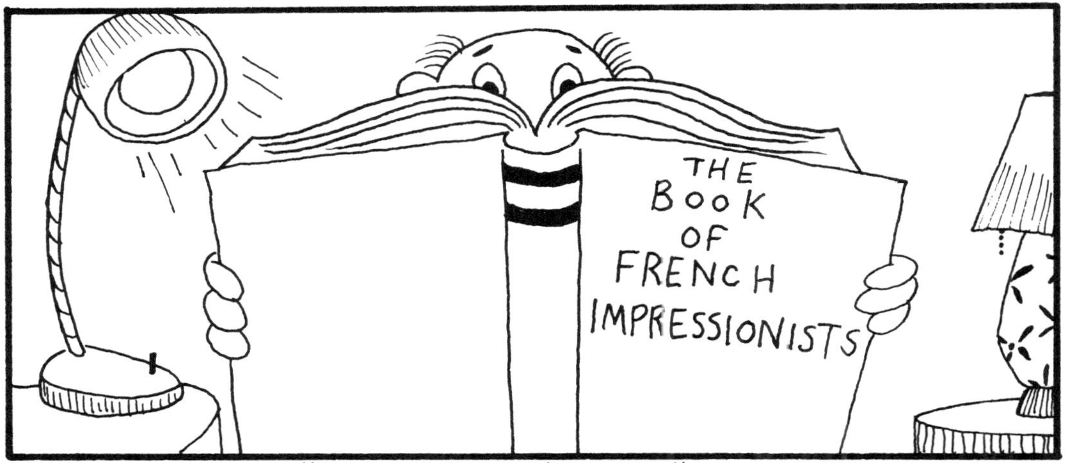
THE BOOK OF FRENCH IMPRESSIONISTS

created by Robert Boxer M.D. Illustrated by Darnell Towns

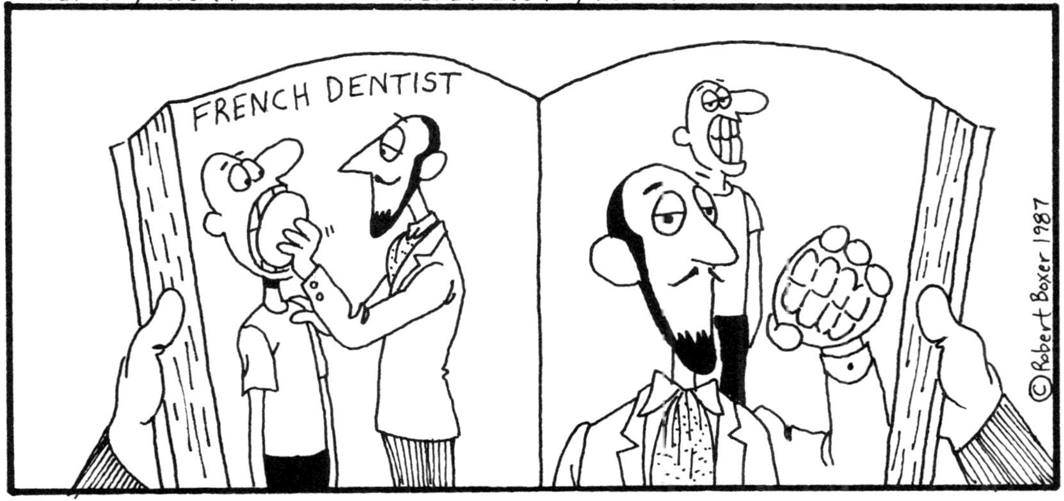
FRENCH DENTIST
© Robert Boxer 1987

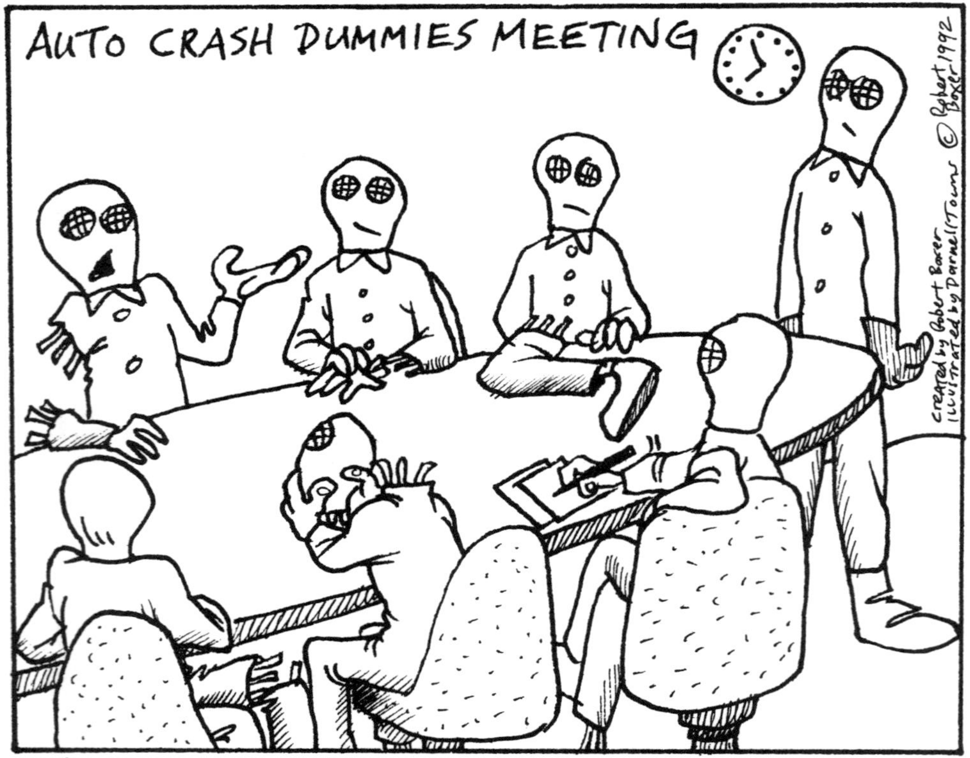
AUTO CRASH DUMMIES MEETING
created by Robert Boxer
illustrated by Darnell Towns
© Robert Boxer 1992

"Are we sure that Dummy Corporations are legal in this state."

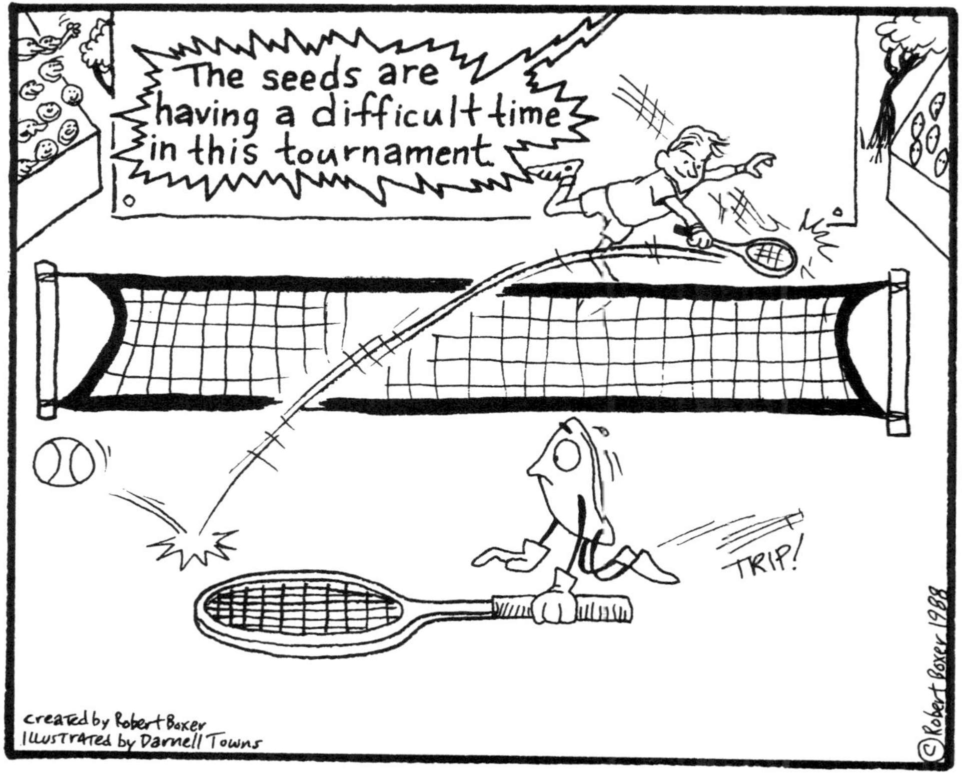
The seeds are having a difficult time in this tournament.
TRIP!
created by Robert Boxer
Illustrated by Darnell Towns
©Robert Boxer 1988

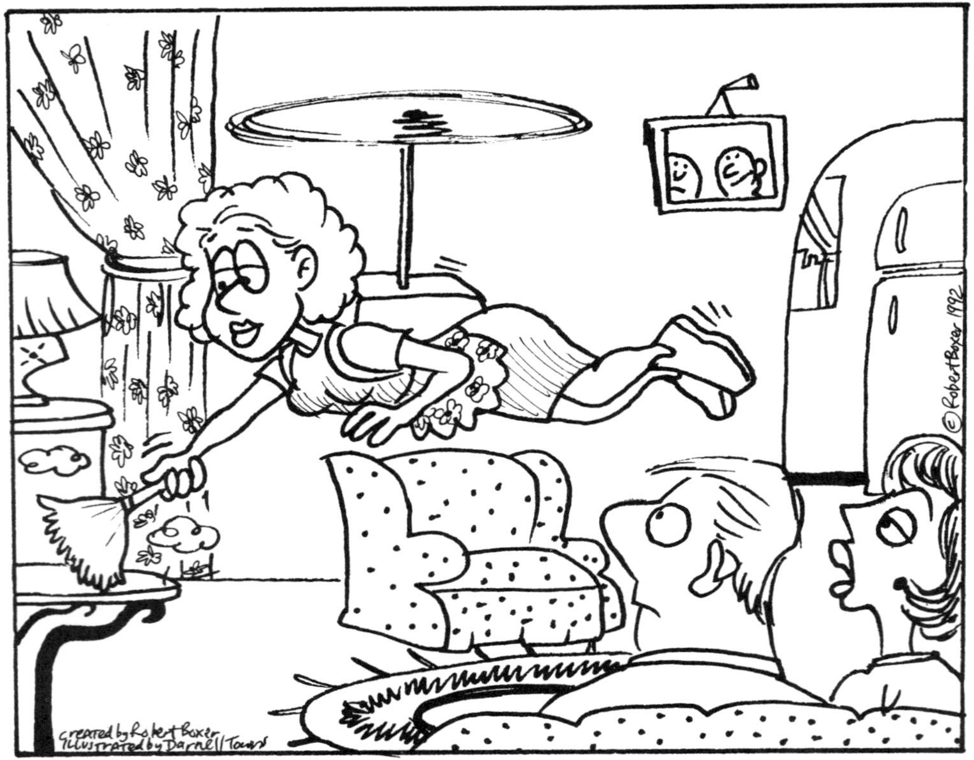
Created by Robert Boxer
Illustrated by Darnell Towns
© Robert Boxer 1992

"I TOLD YOU, NOTHING, ABSOLUTELY NOTHING IS BENEATH HER."

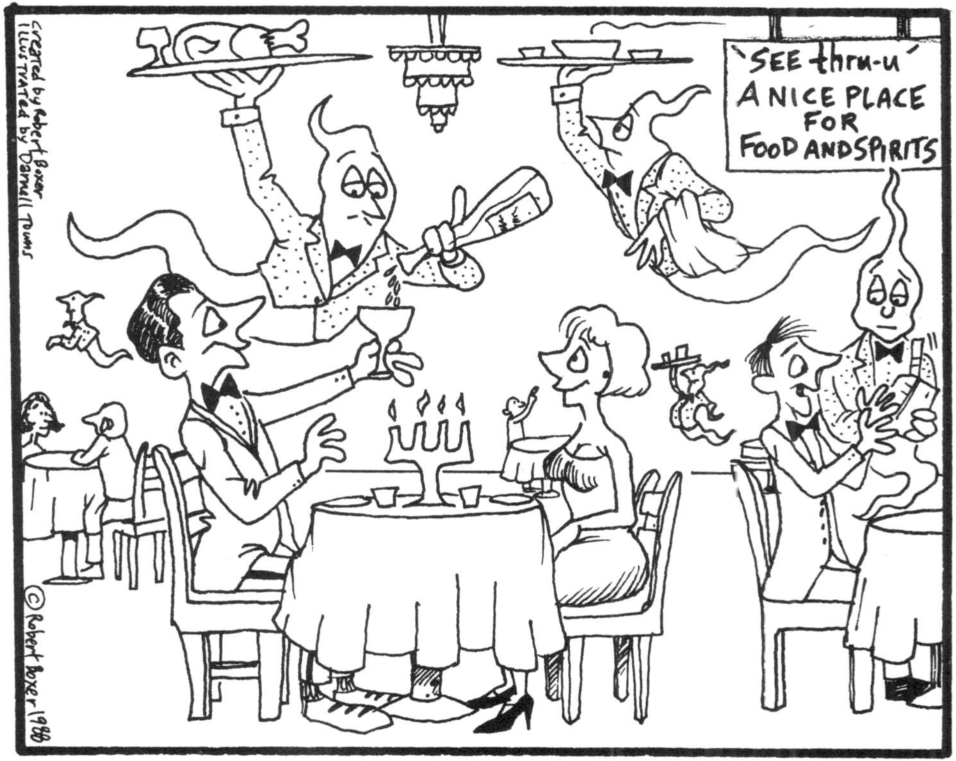

"SEE thru-u"
A NICE PLACE
FOR
FOOD AND SPIRITS
created by Robert Boxer
illustrated by Darnell Towns
© Robert Boxer 1988

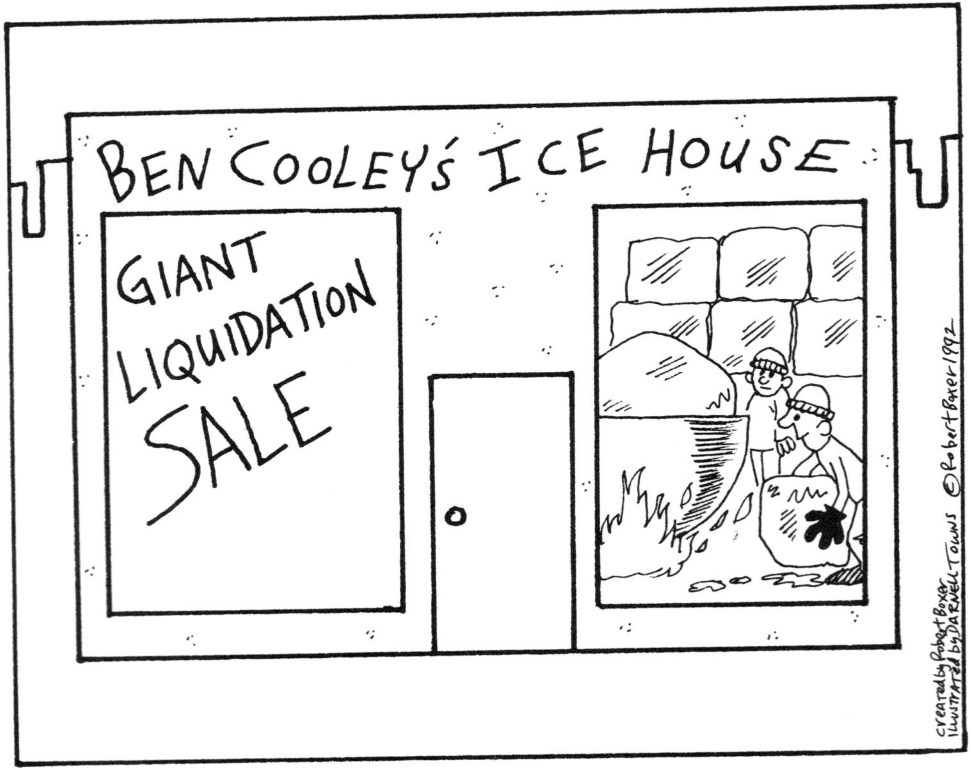
BEN COOLEY'S ICE HOUSE
GIANT LIQUIDATION SALE
created by Robert Boxer
Illustrated by DARNELL TOWNS ©Robert Boxer 1992

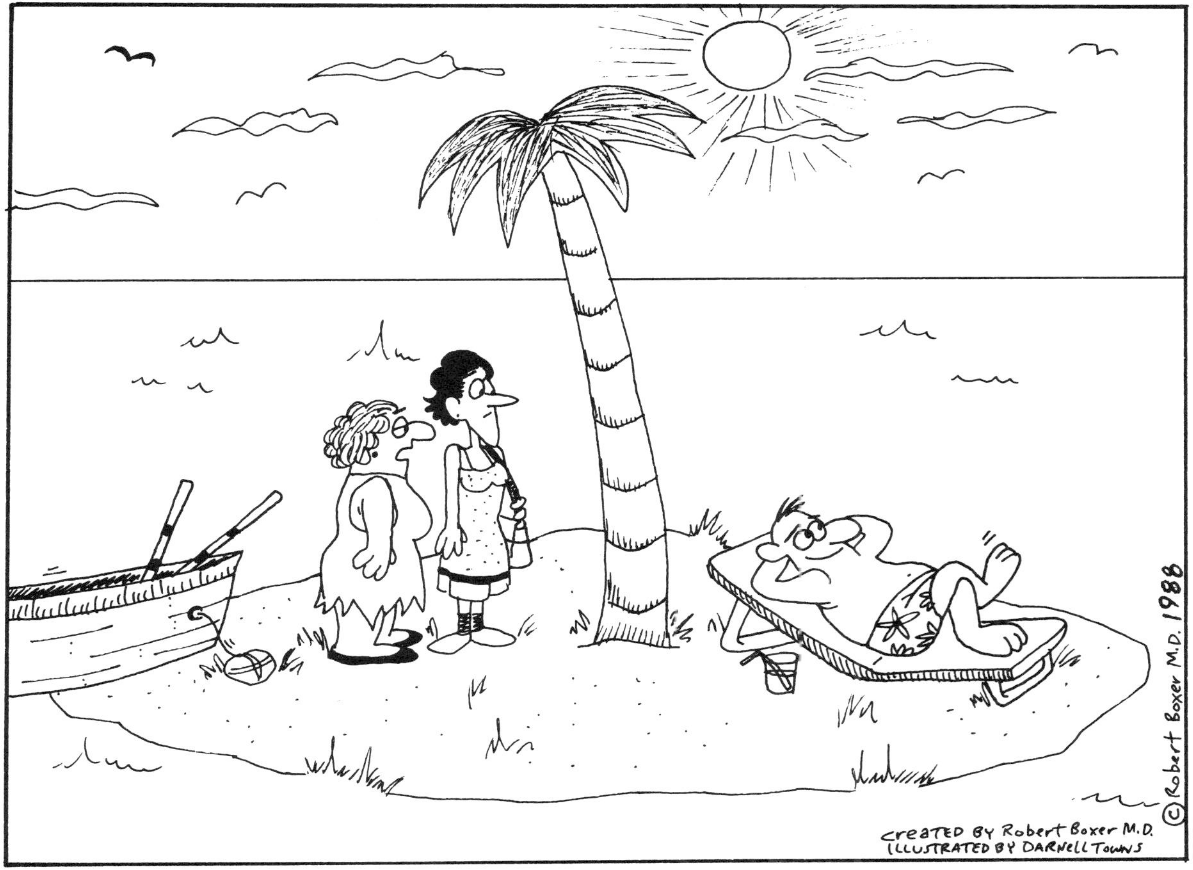
©Robert Boxer M.D. 1988
CREATED BY Robert Boxer M.D.
ILLUSTRATED BY DARNELL TOWNS

"My Husband asked for Aisle seats so often, he decided to get a permanent one".

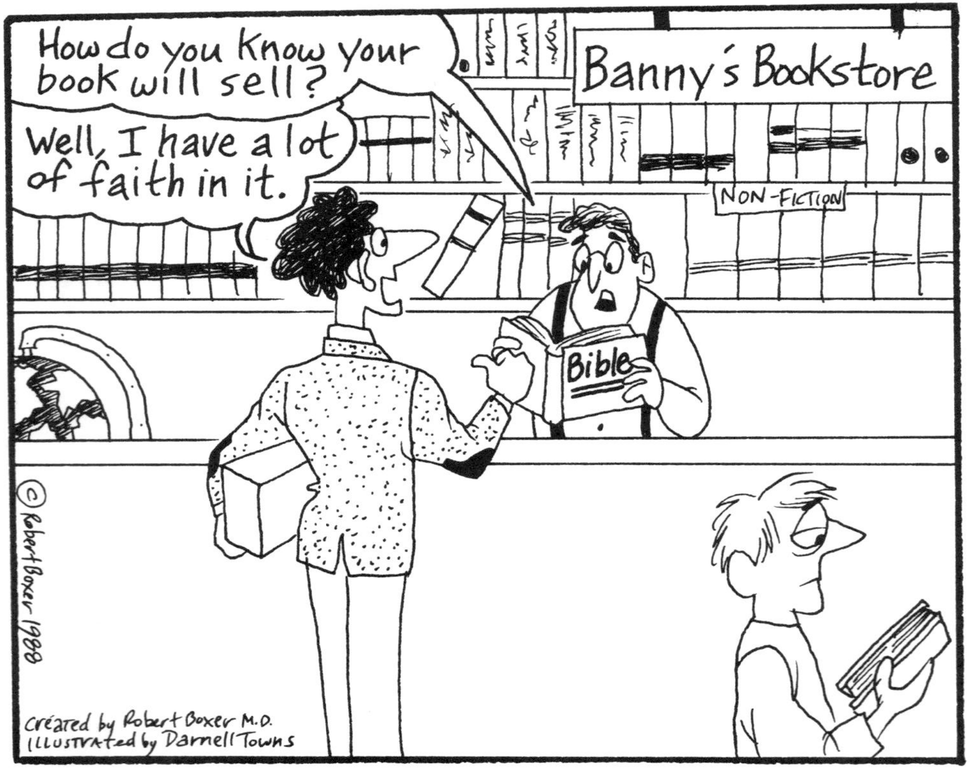
How do you know your book will sell?
Well, I have a lot of faith in it.
Banny's Bookstore
NON-FICTION
Bible
© Robert Boxer 1988
Created by Robert Boxer M.D.
Illustrated by Darnell Towns

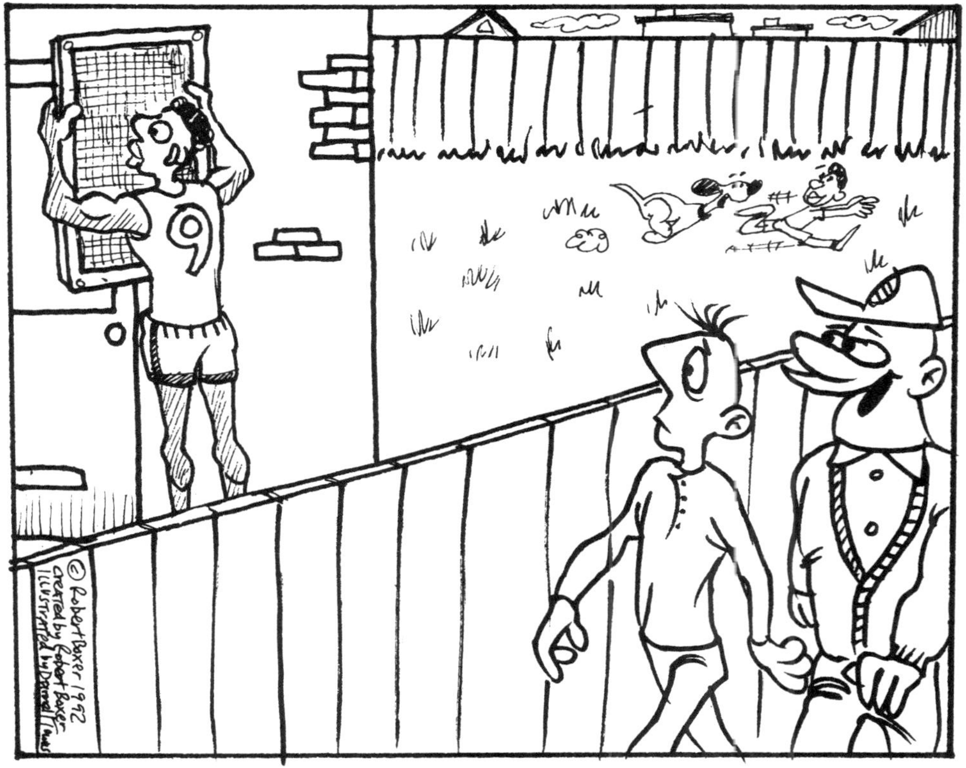
© Robert Baxer 1992
created by Robert Baxer

"There's our star Basketball player. As always he's setting a SCREEN.

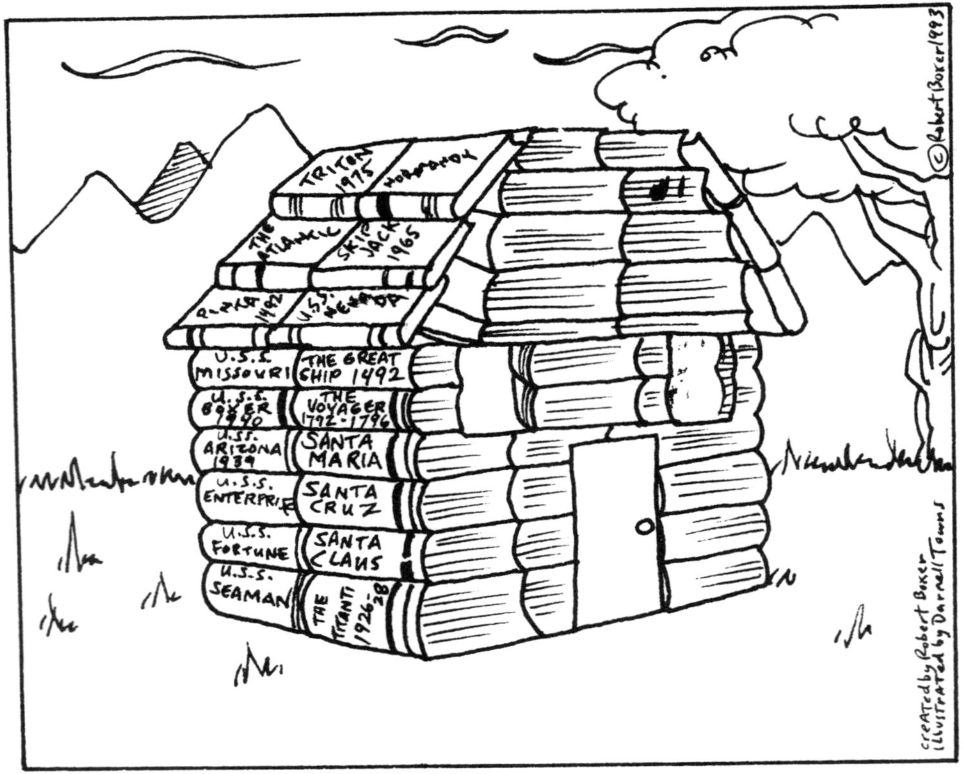
TRITON 1975
NORMANDY
THE ATLANTIC
SKIP JACK 1965
PINTA 1492
U.S.S.
U.S.S. MISSOURI
THE GREAT SHIP 1492
U.S.S. BOXER 1940
THE VOYAGER 1792-1796
U.S.S. ARIZONA 1939
SANTA MARIA
U.S.S. ENTERPRISE
SANTA CRUZ
U.S.S. FORTUNE
SANTA CLAUS
U.S.S. SEAMAN
THE TITANTI 1926-28
©Robert Boxer 1993
created by Robert Boxer
illustrated by Darnell Towns

LOG CABIN

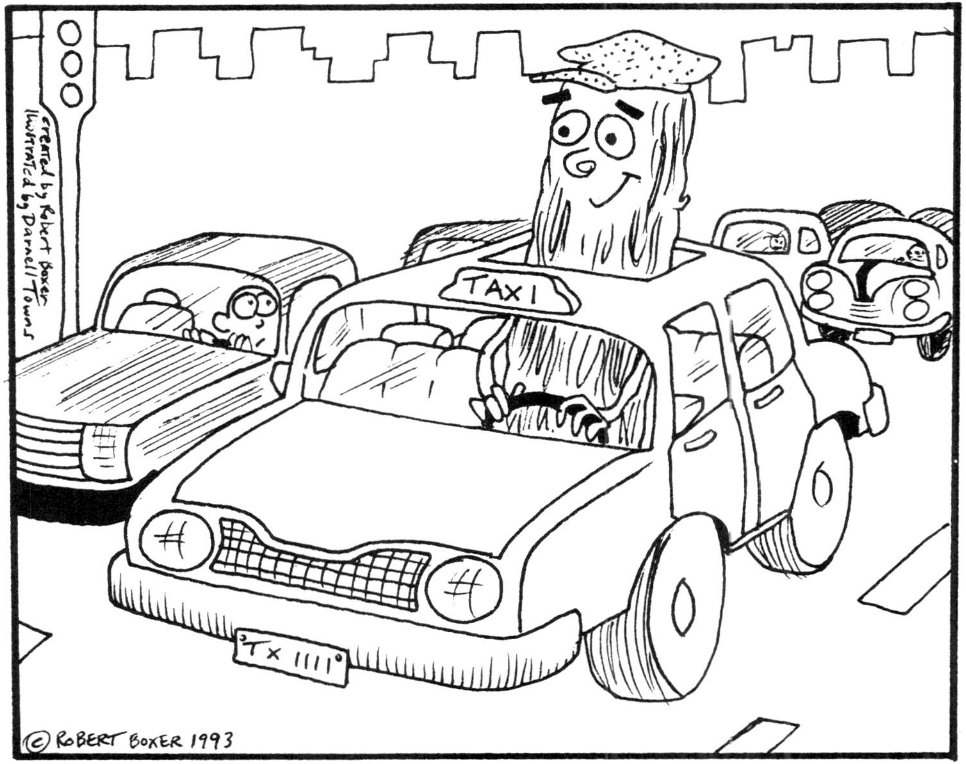
created by Robert Boxer
Illustrated by Darnell Towns
TAXI
TX 1111
© ROBERT BOXER 1993

ANOTHER LOG CABBIN'.

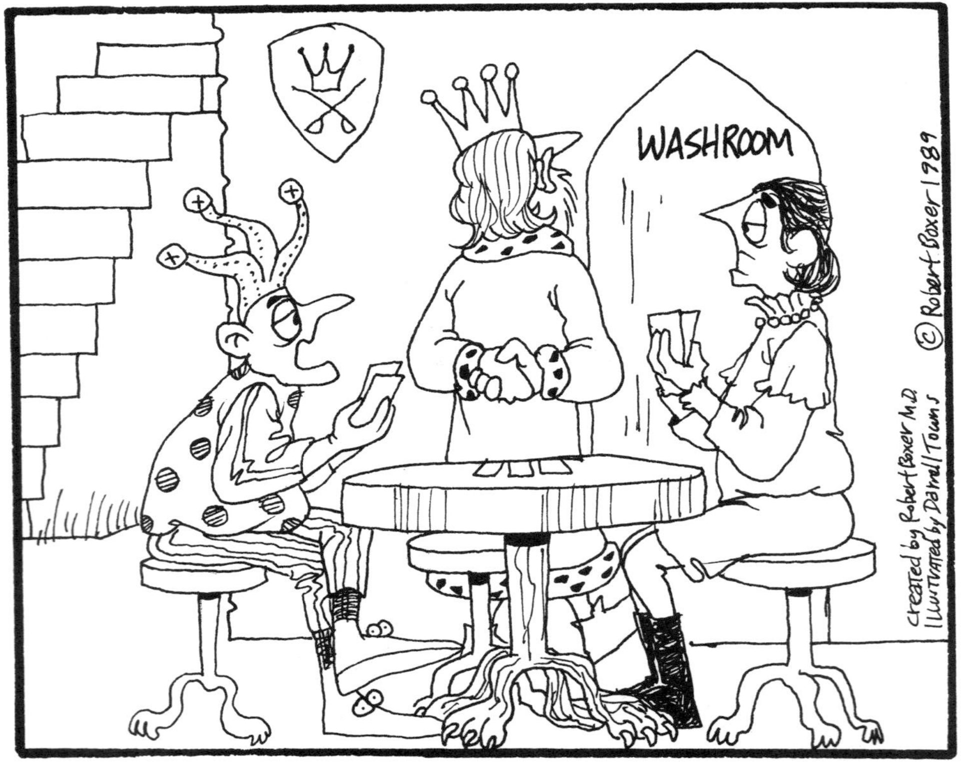
WASHROOM
© Robert Boxer 1989
created by Robert Boxer M.D.
Illustrated by Darrell Towns

"I think I sense a Royal flush."

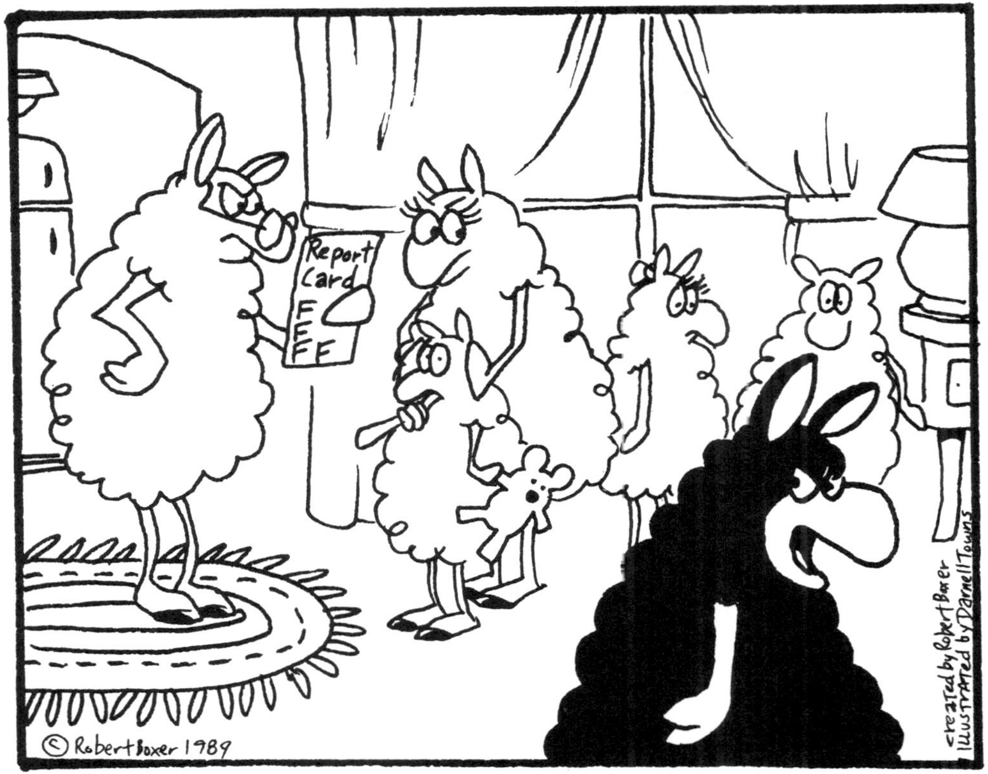
Report Card
F
F
F
F
© Robert Boxer 1989
created by Robert Boxer
ILLUSTRATED by Darnell Towns

"I don't even want to go to college."

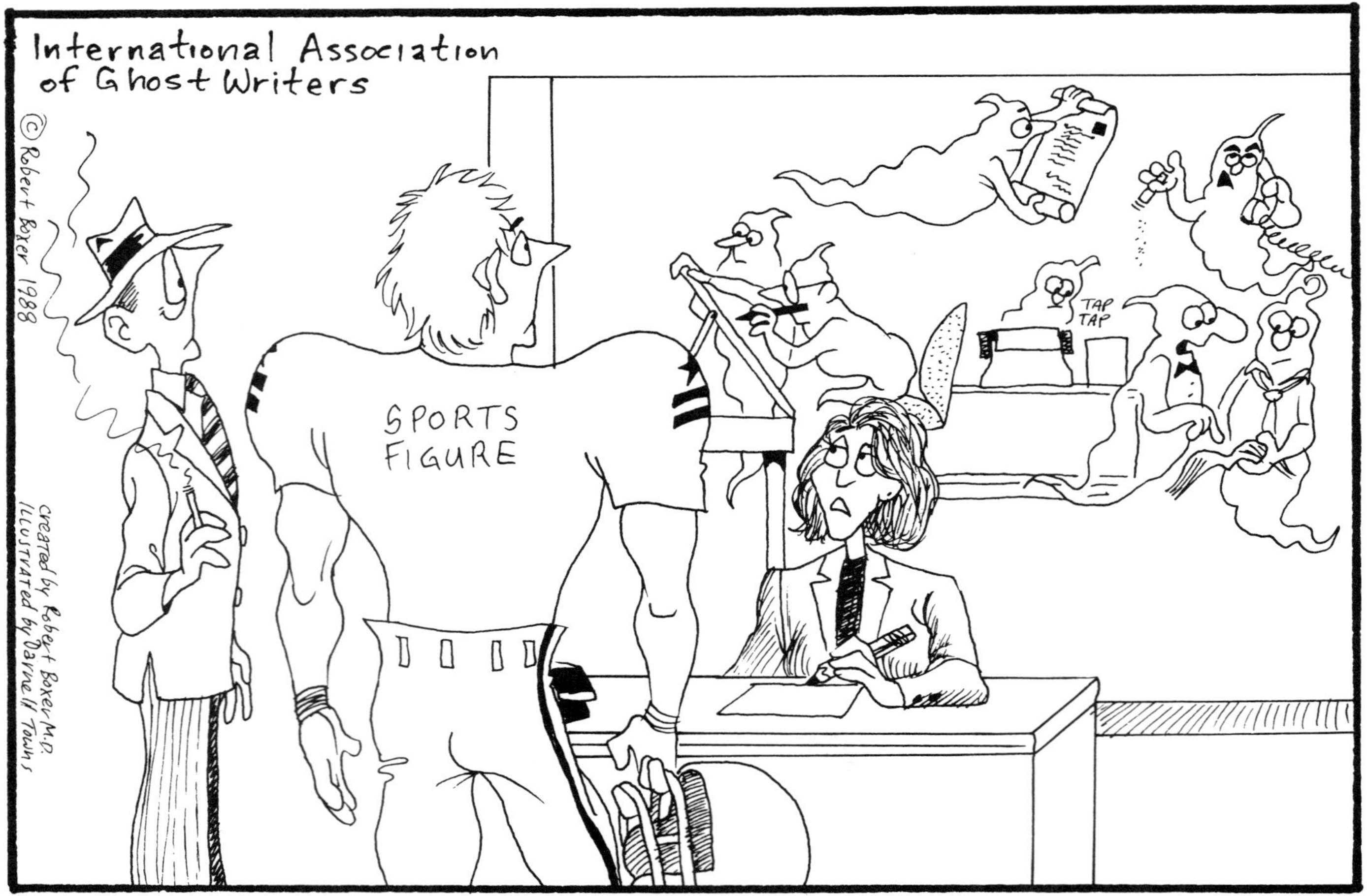

International Association
of Ghost Writers
© Robert Boxer 1988
SPORTS
FIGURE
TAP
TAP
created by Robert Boxer M.D.
Illustrated by Darnell Towns

"May I help you?"

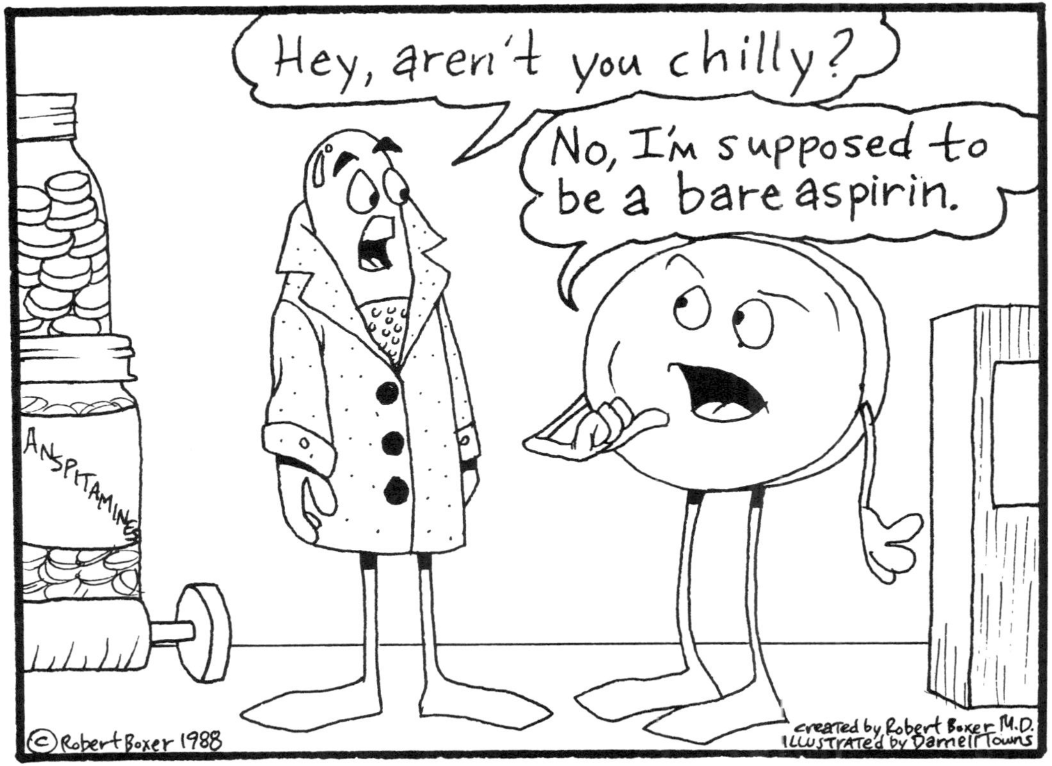
Hey, aren't you chilly?
No, I'm supposed to be a bare aspirin.
ANSPITAMINES
© Robert Boxer 1988
created by Robert Boxer M.D.
ILLUSTRATED by Darnell Towns

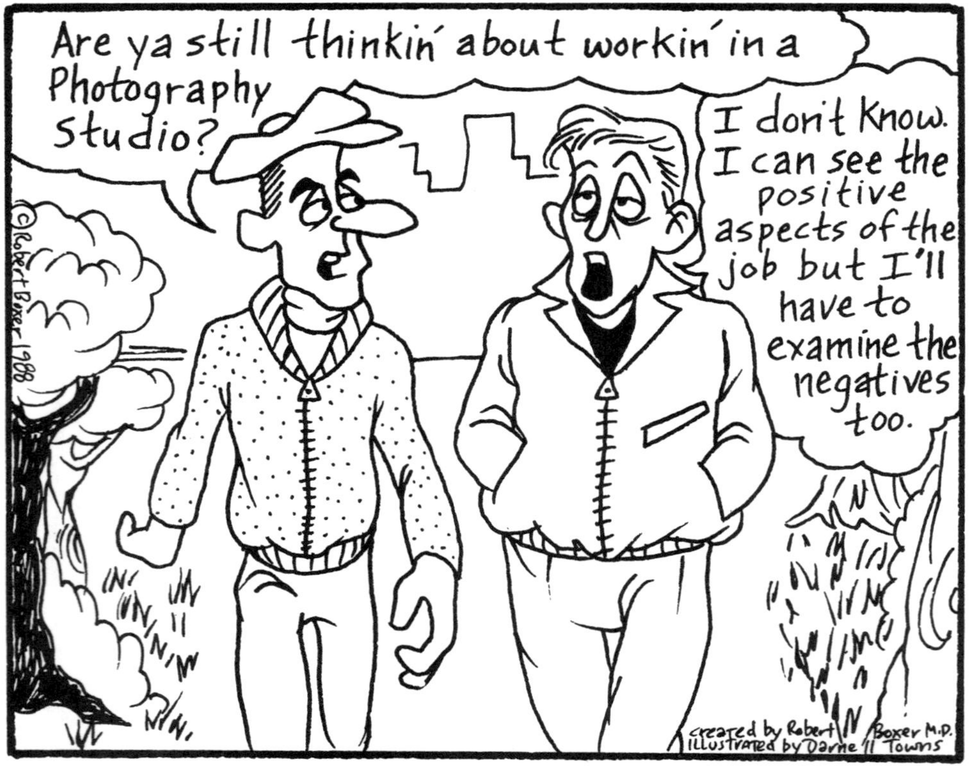
Are ya still thinkin' about workin' in a Photography studio?
I don't know. I can see the positive aspects of the job but I'll have to examine the negatives too.
©Robert Boxer 1988
created by Robert Boxer M.D.
illustrated by Darnell Towns

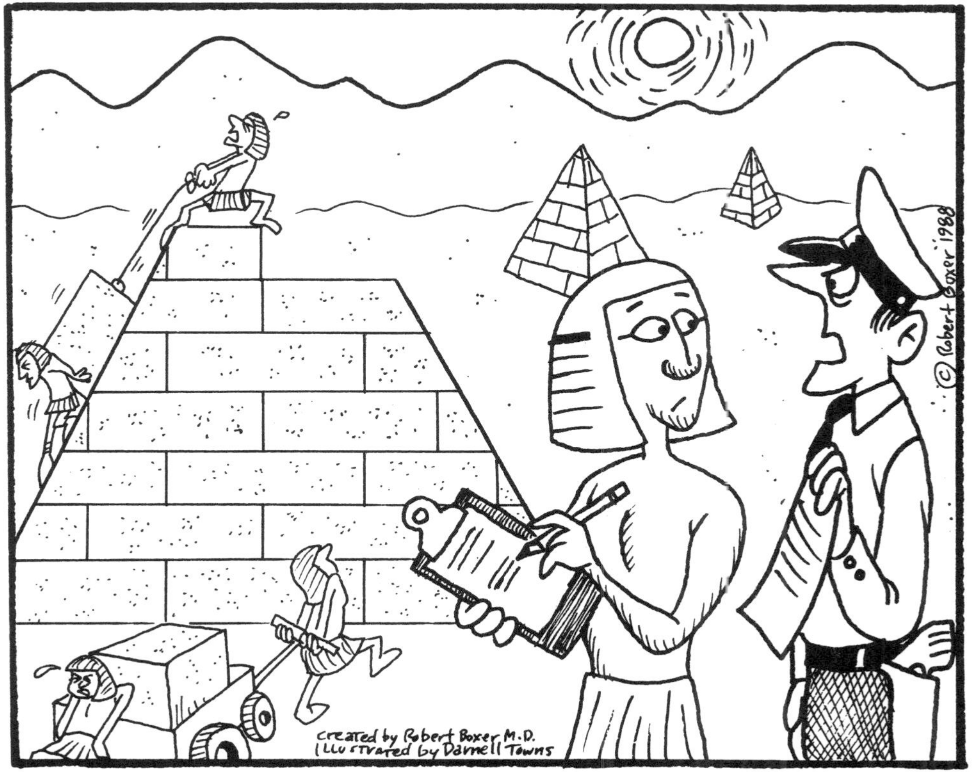
© Robert Boxer 1988
created by Robert Boxer M.D.
Illustrated by Darnell Towns

"Mr. Foreman, I have a warrant for your arrest. You've been charged with being involved in a pyramid scheme."

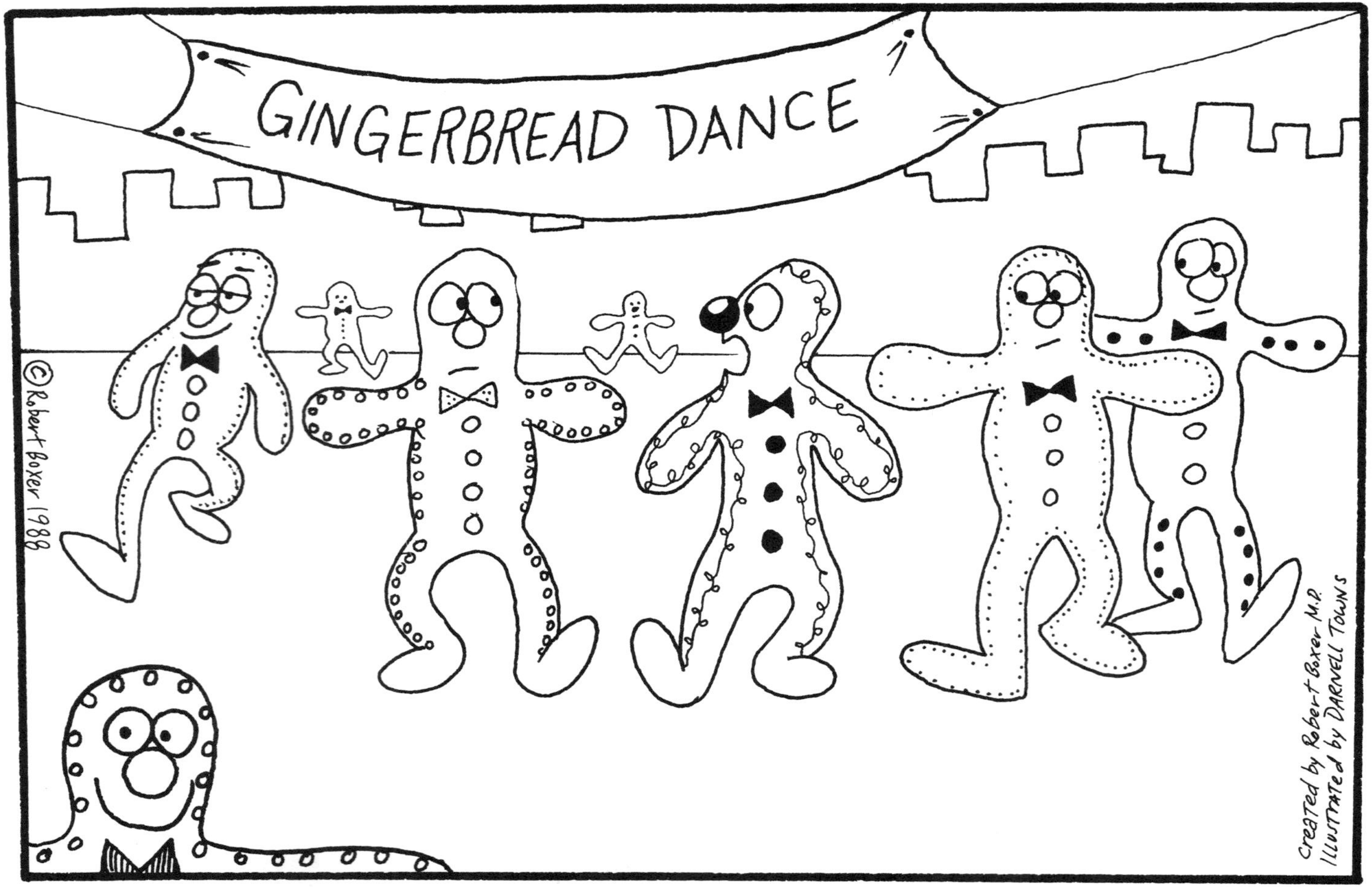
GINGERBREAD DANCE
©Robert Boxer 1988
Created by Robert Boxer M.D.
Illustrated by DARNELL TOWNS

"I just don't want to get involved with a Stalemate."

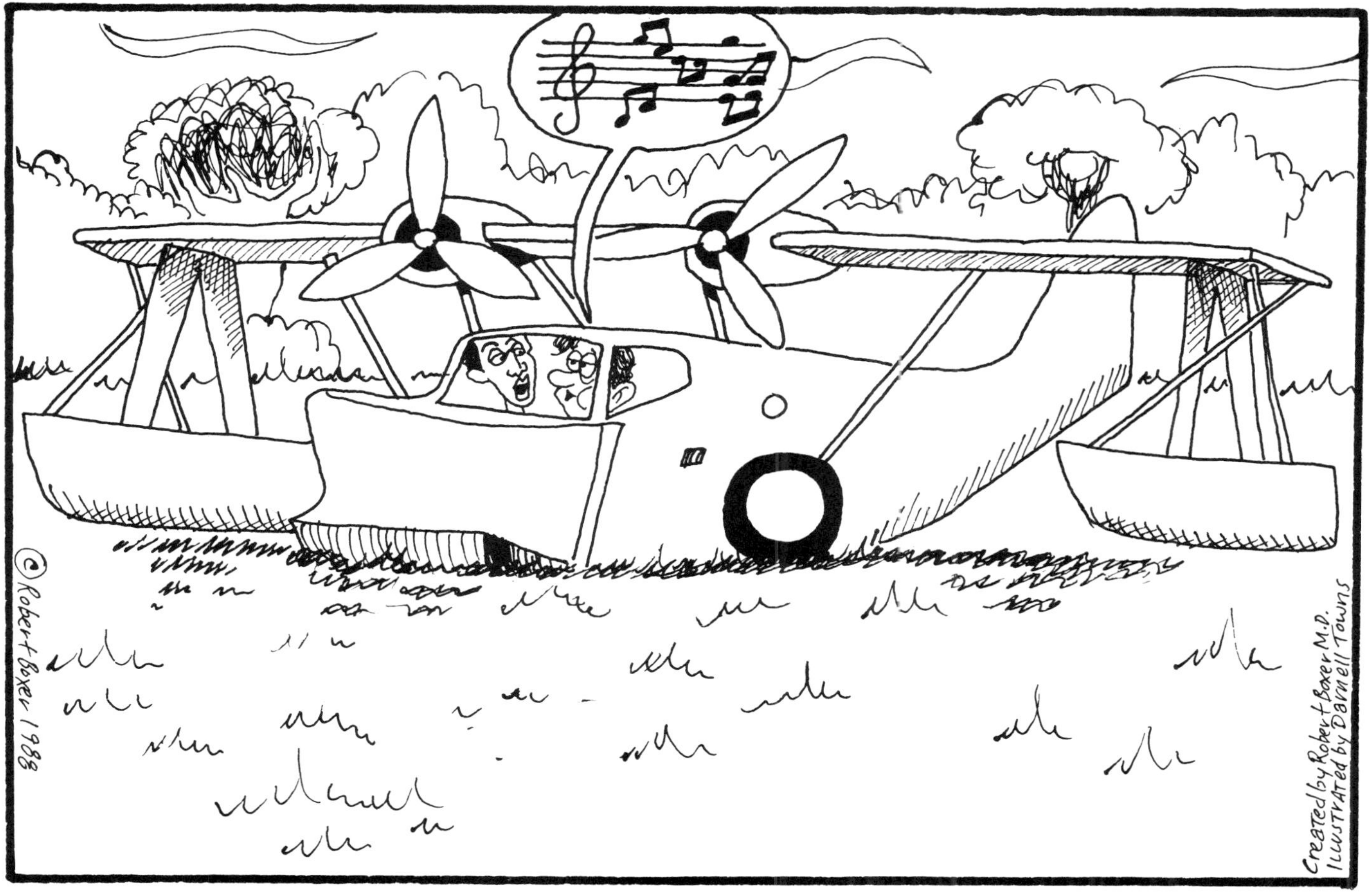
© Robert Boxer 1988
Created by Robert Boxer M.D.
Illustrated by Darnell Towns

"Bob, I sure hope your **pun tunes** keep us afloat".

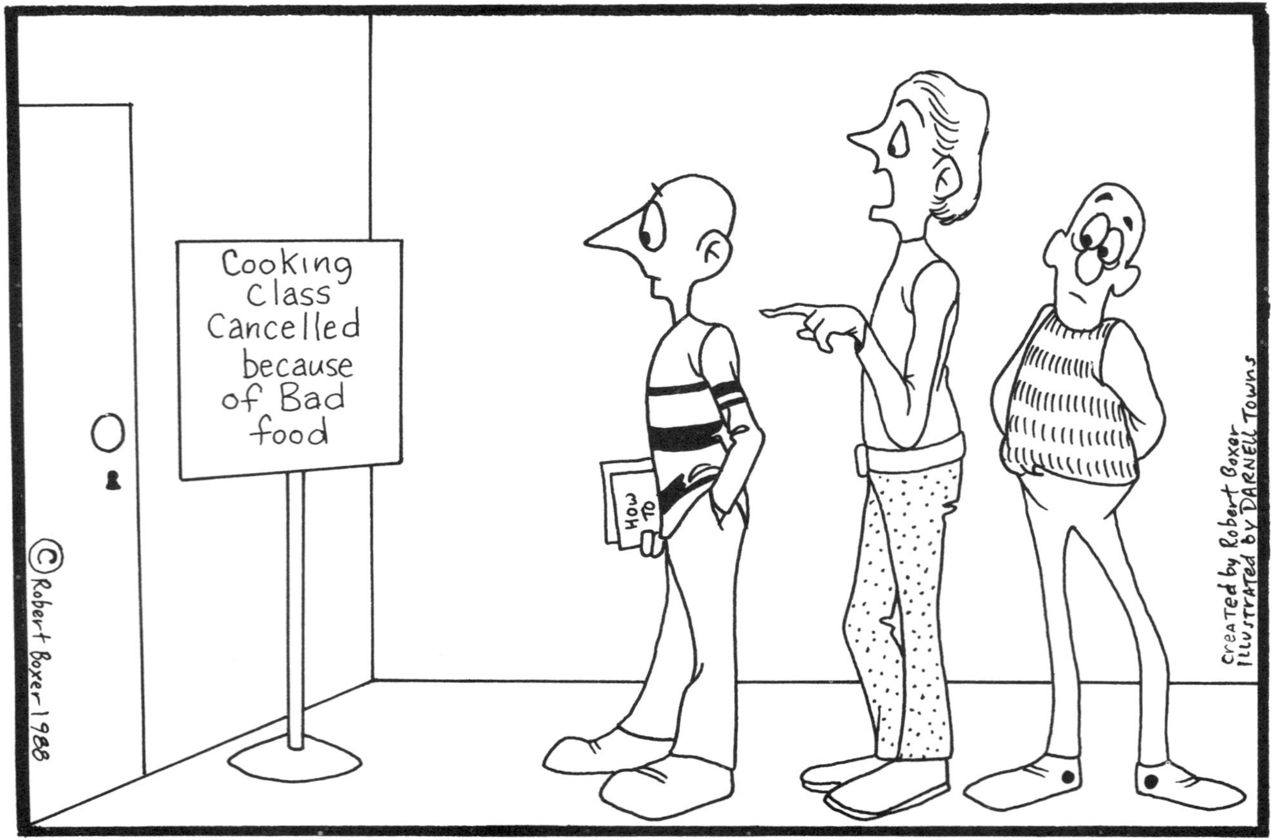
Cooking Class Cancelled because of Bad food
HOW TO
© Robert Boxer-1988
CREATED by Robert Boxer
ILLUSTRATED BY DARNELL TOWNS

"It's not only Poor taste, but absolutely no class."

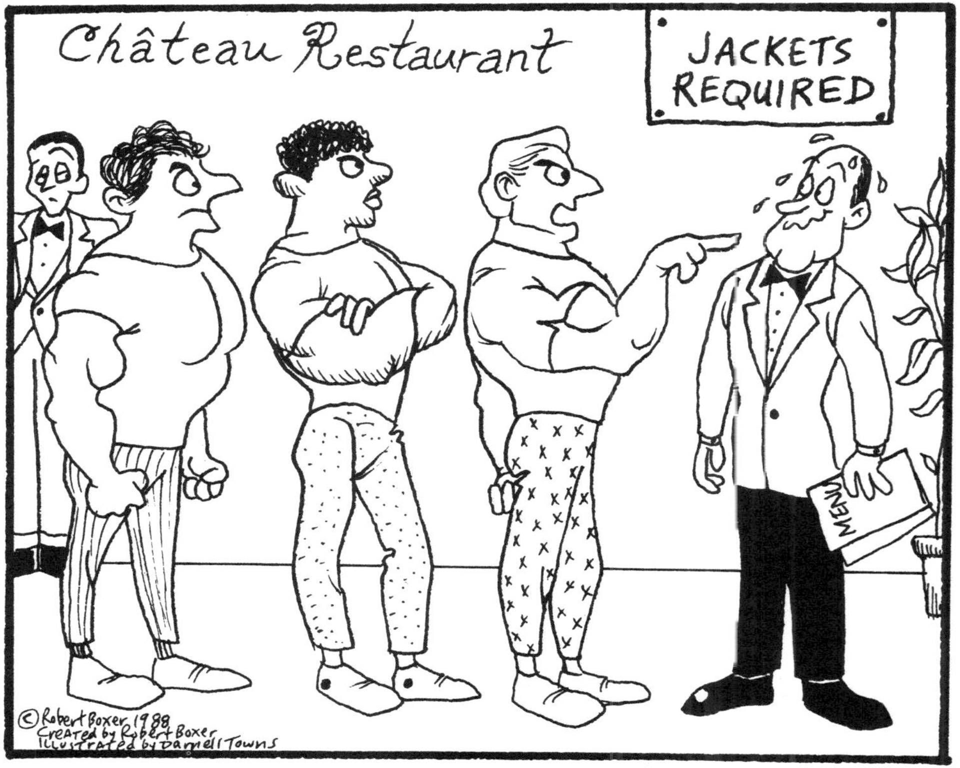
Château Restaurant
JACKETS REQUIRED
MENU
©Robert Boxer 1988
Created by Robert Boxer
Illustrated by Darnell Towns

"We thought the second amendment guarantees us the right to bare ARMS."

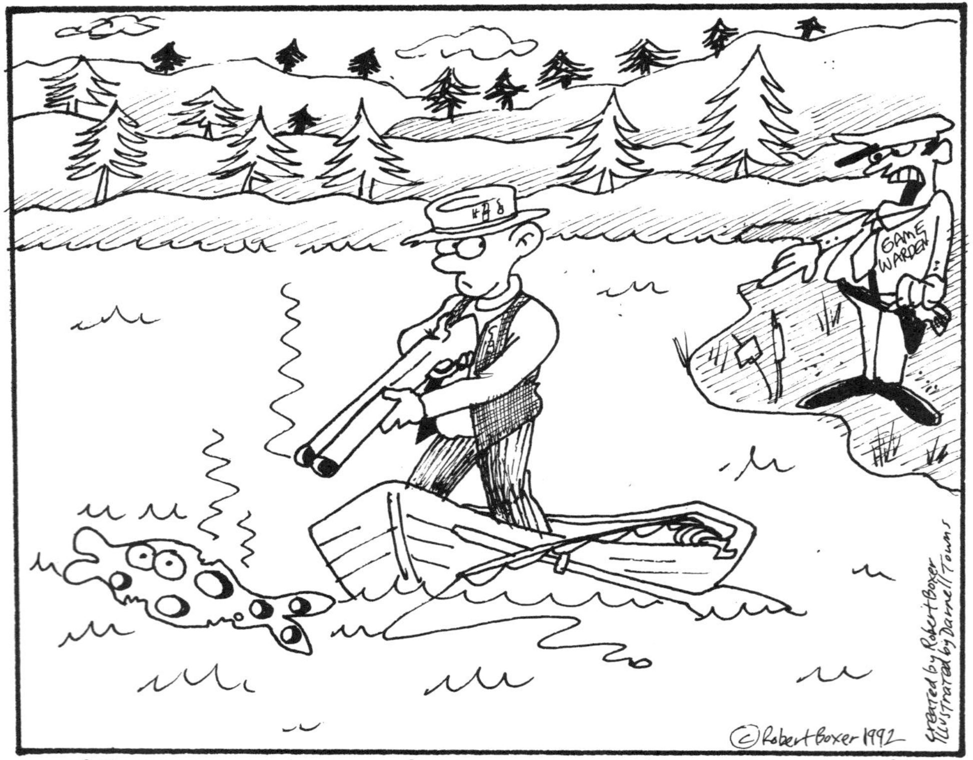
GAME WARDEN
©Robert Boxer 1992
Created by Robert Boxer
Illustrated by Darnell Towns

"HOLY MACKEREL! You know that's illegal!"

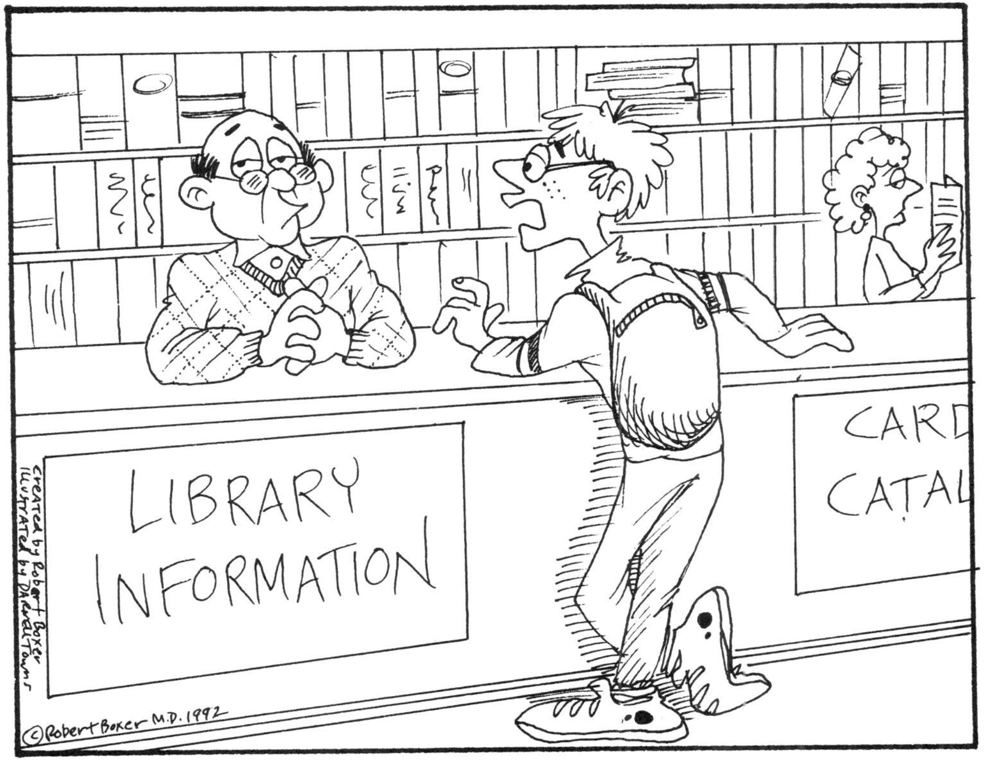
LIBRARY INFORMATION
CARD CATAL
CREATED by Robert Boxer
ILLUSTRATED by Darrell Towns
©Robert Boxer M.D. 1992

"EXCUSE ME, I'M TRYING TO FIND OUT ABOUT HENRY FORD AND LEE IACOCCA. DO YOU HAVE A SECTION ON **AUTO**BIOGRAPHIES?"

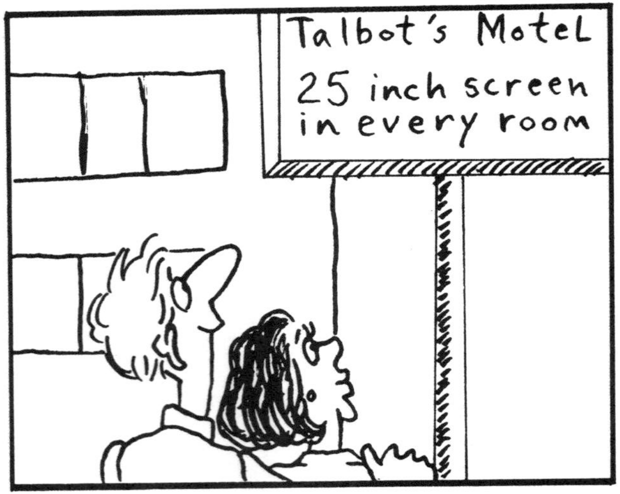
Talbot's MoteL
25 inch screen
in every room

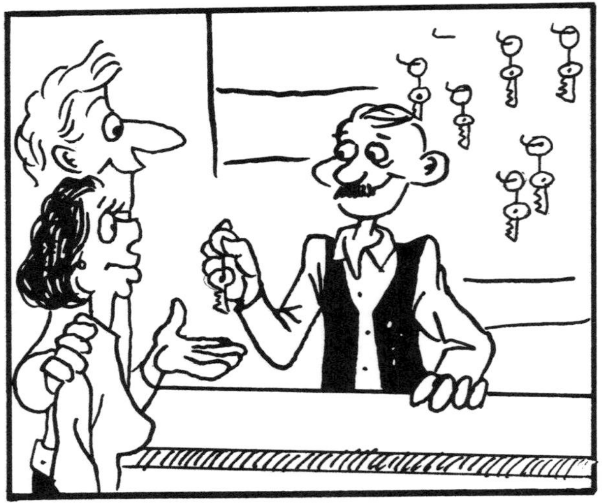

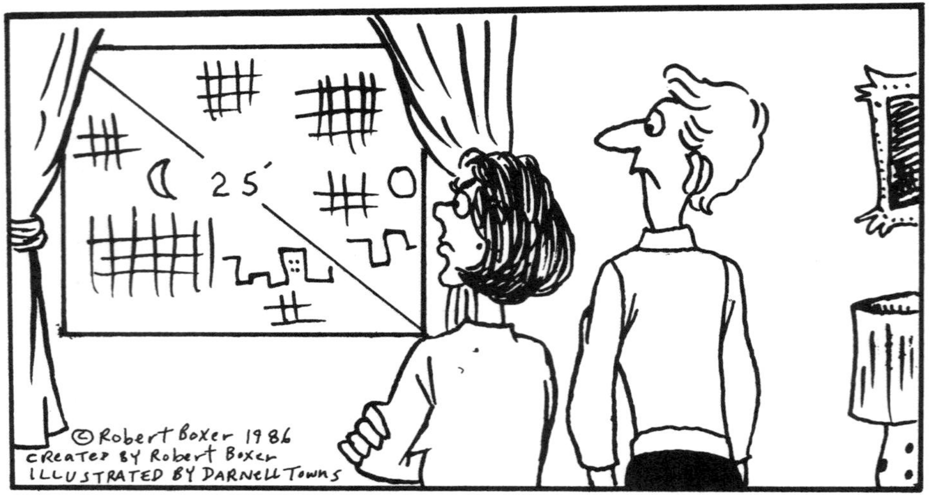
25'
©Robert Boxer 1986
CREATED BY Robert Boxer
ILLUSTRATED BY DARNELL TOWNS

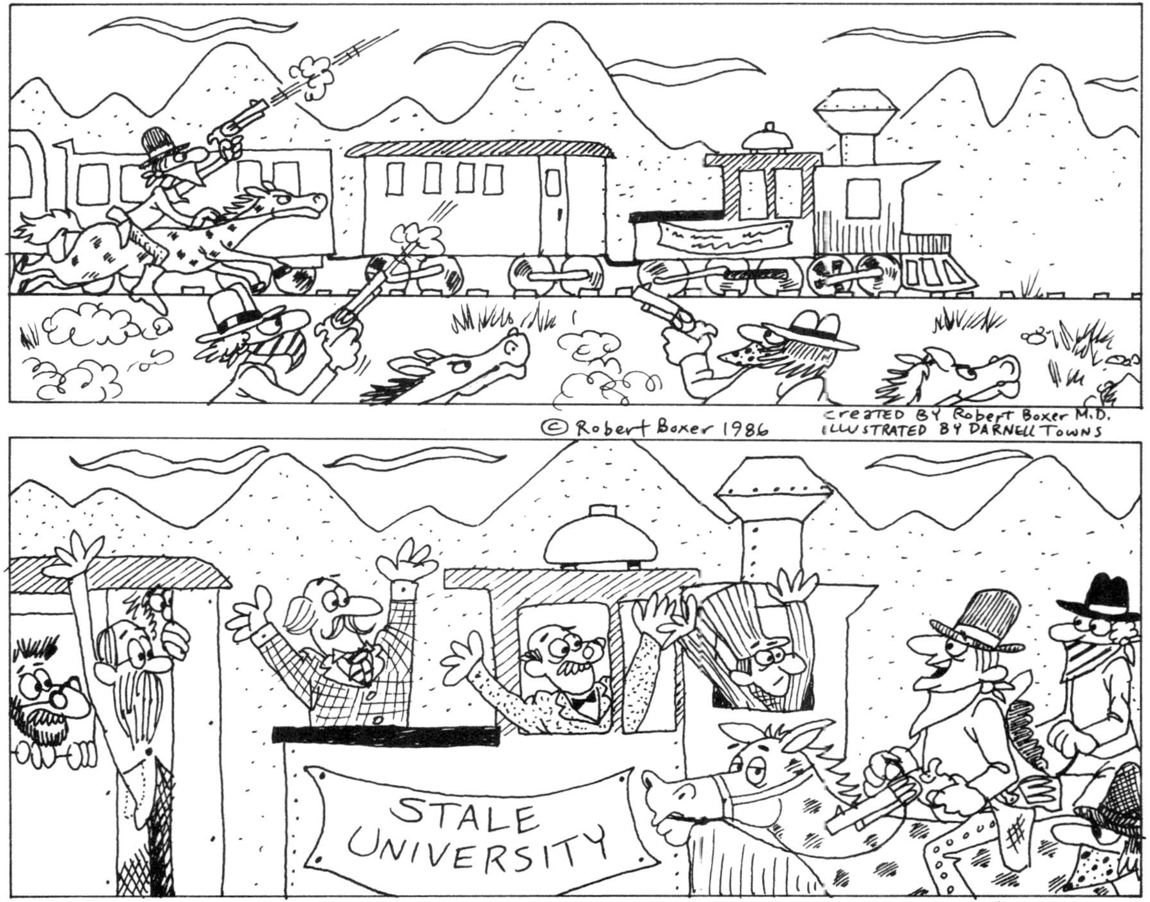
© Robert Boxer 1986
Created by Robert Boxer M.D.
Illustrated by Darnell Towns
STALE
UNIVERSITY

"Sorry to interrupt your train of thought".

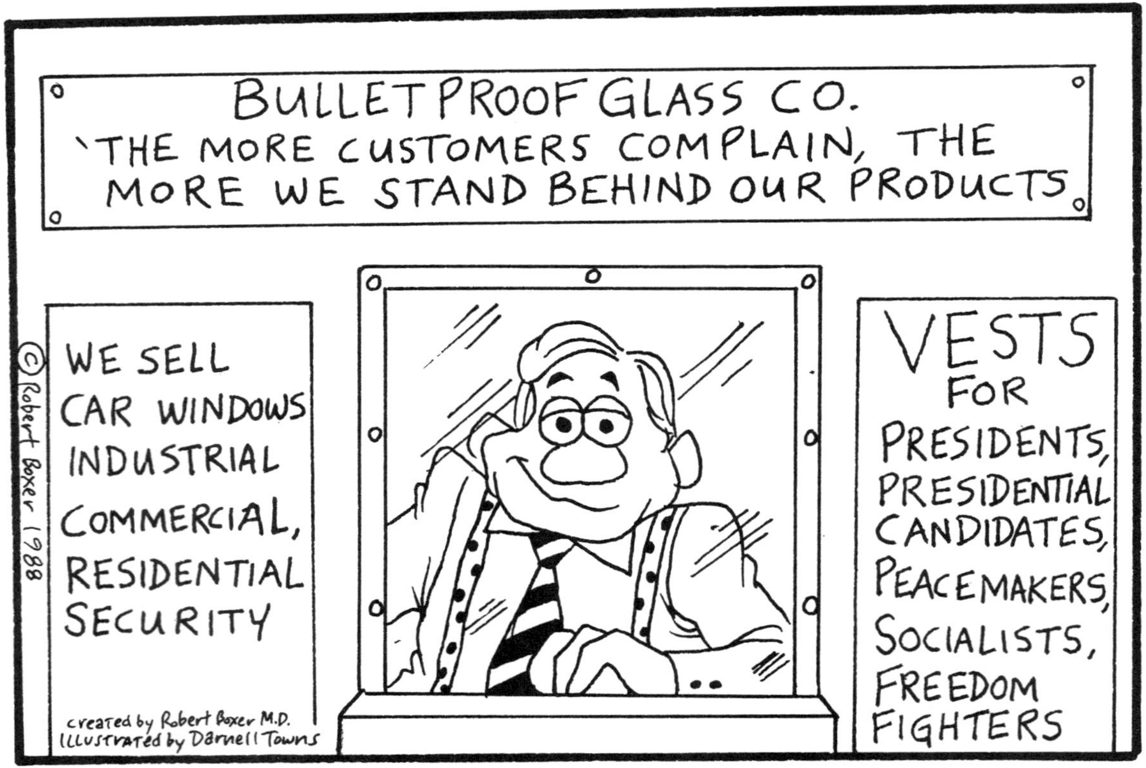
BULLET PROOF GLASS CO.
`THE MORE CUSTOMERS COMPLAIN, THE MORE WE STAND BEHIND OUR PRODUCTS'
WE SELL CAR WINDOWS INDUSTRIAL COMMERCIAL, RESIDENTIAL SECURITY
VESTS FOR PRESIDENTS, PRESIDENTIAL CANDIDATES, PEACEMAKERS, SOCIALISTS, FREEDOM FIGHTERS
© Robert Boxer 1988
created by Robert Boxer M.D.
illustrated by Darnell Towns

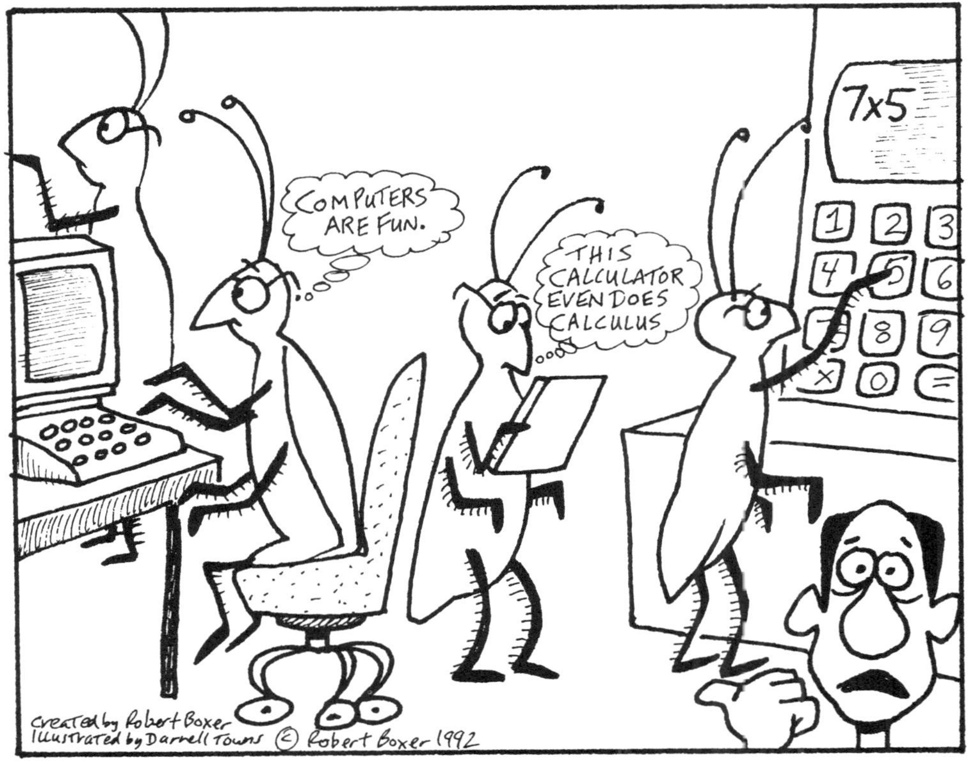
COMPUTERS ARE FUN.
THIS CALCULATOR EVEN DOES CALCULUS
7x5
1 2 3
4 5 6
7 8 9
x 0 =
CREATED by Robert Boxer
Illustrated by Darnell Towns © Robert Boxer 1992

"NO WONDER ROACHES MULTIPLY SO FAST."

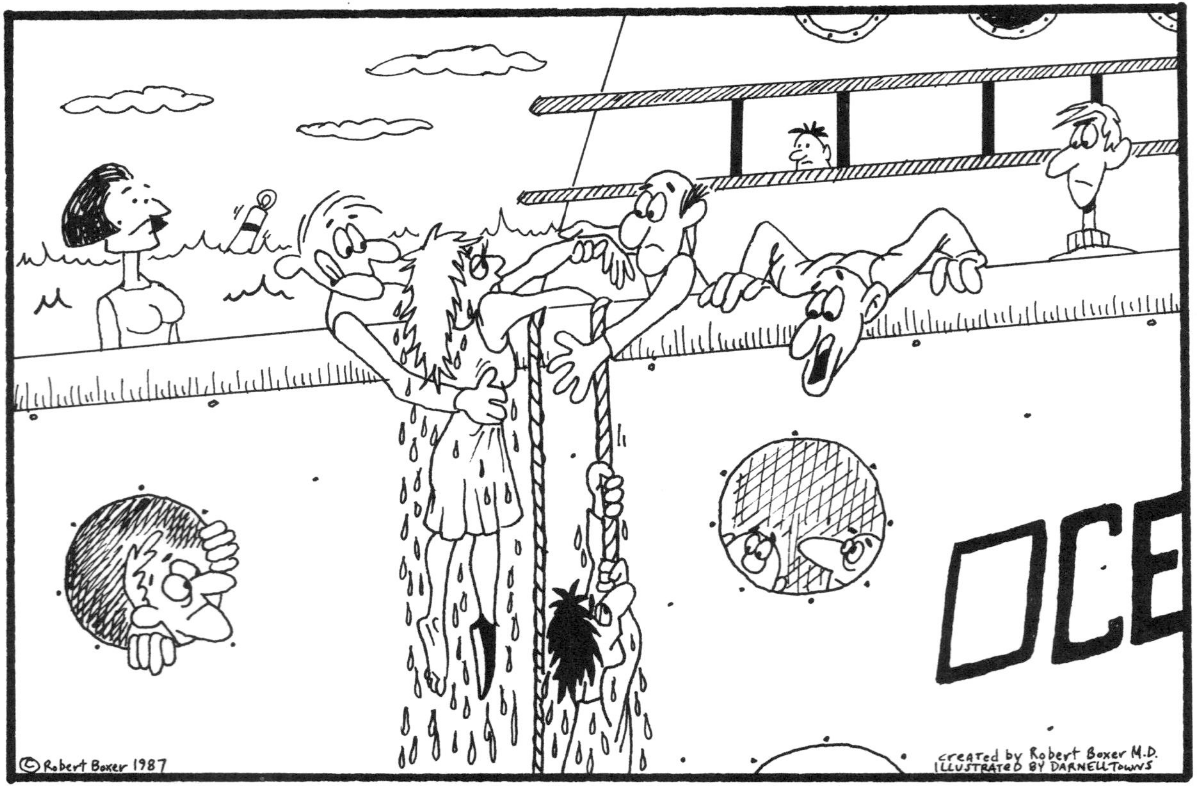

OCE
© Robert Boxer 1987
created by Robert Boxer M.D.
ILLUSTRATED BY DARNELL TOWNS

"You were'nt joking when you said that you go overboard for blondes."

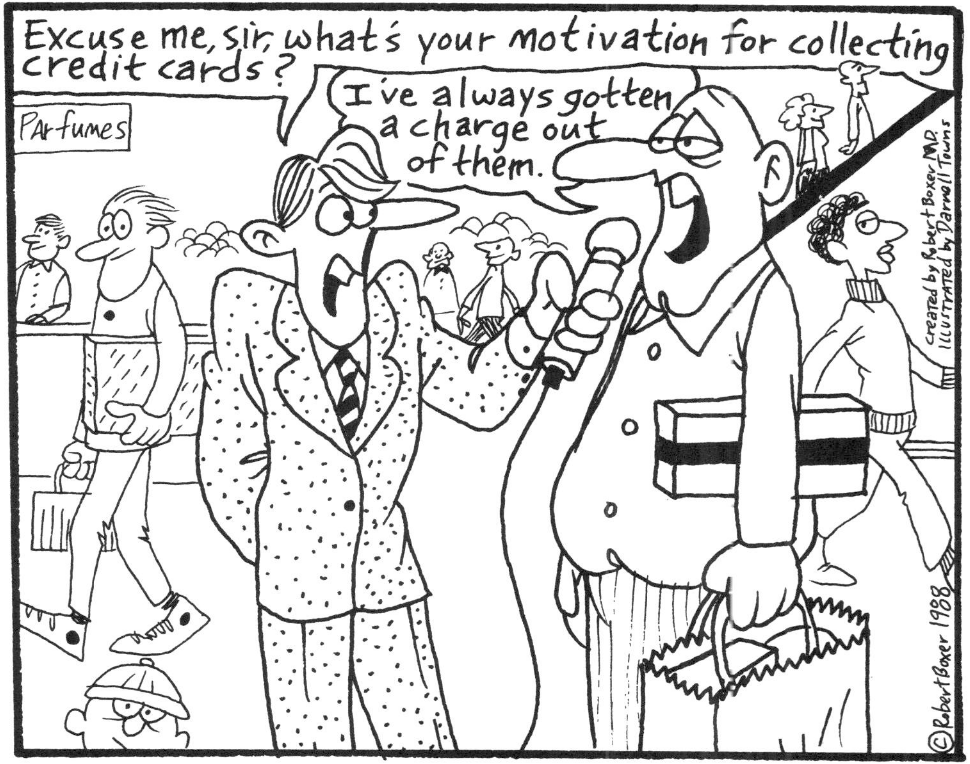
Excuse me, sir, what's your motivation for collecting credit cards?
I've always gotten a charge out of them.
Parfumes
created by Robert Boxer M.D.
ILLUSTRATED by Darrell Towns
©Robert Boxer 1988

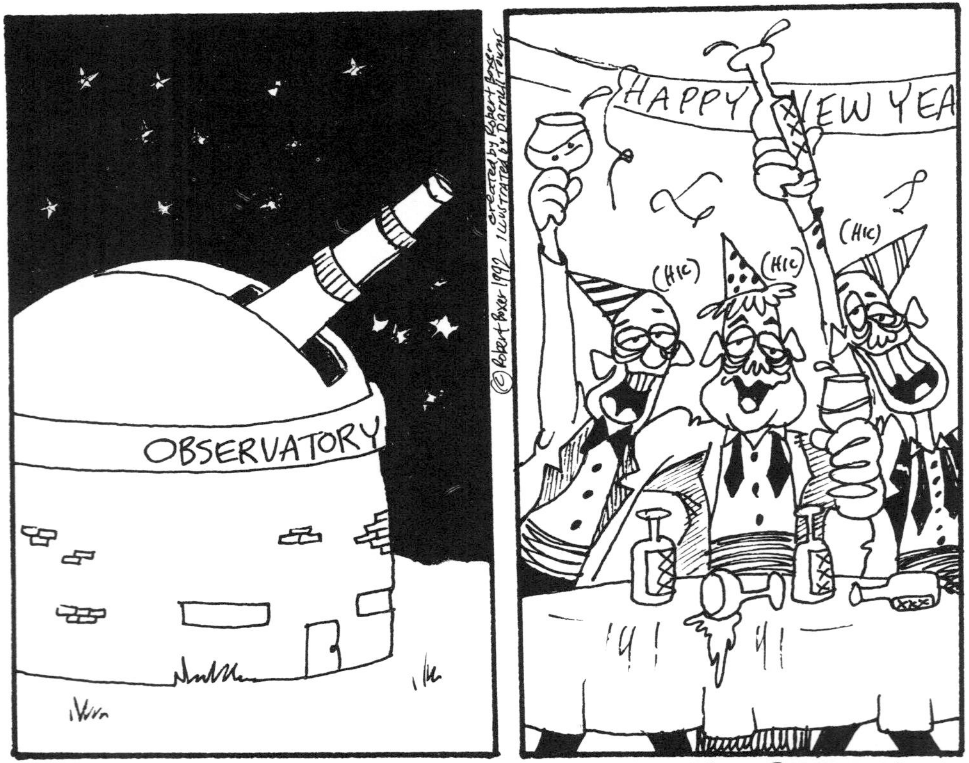
OBSERVATORY
HAPPY NEW YEA
(HIC)
(HIC)
(HIC)

HIGH RESOLUTION THE HIGHEST RESOLUTION.

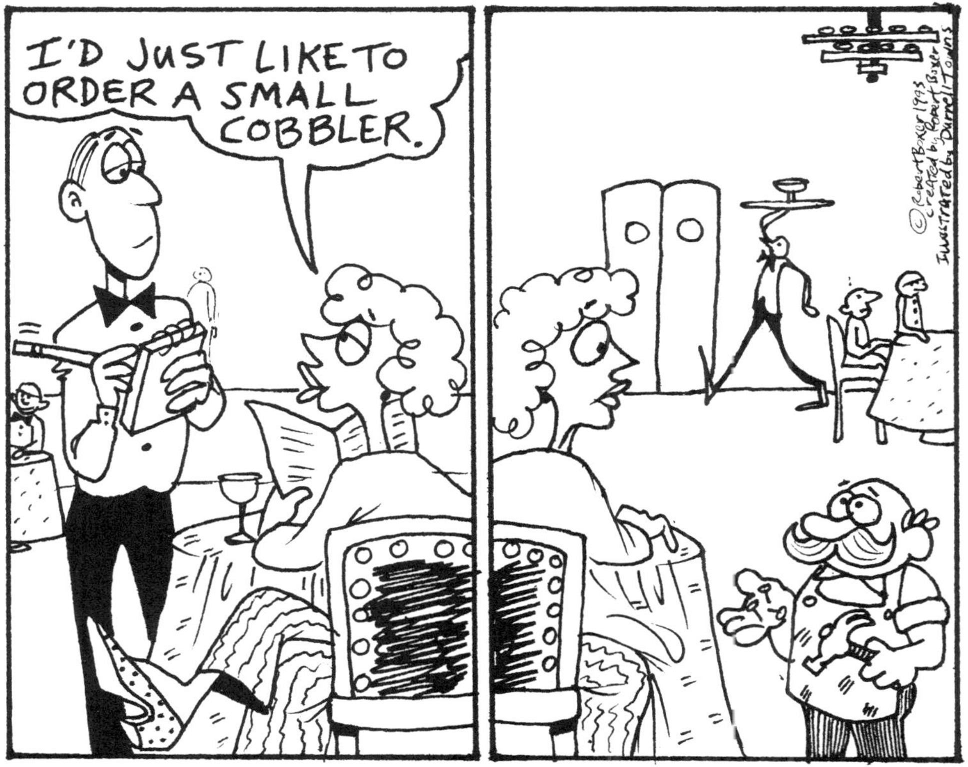
I'D JUST LIKE TO ORDER A SMALL COBBLER.
© Robert Boxer 1993
Created by Robert Boxer
Illustrated by Darnell Towns

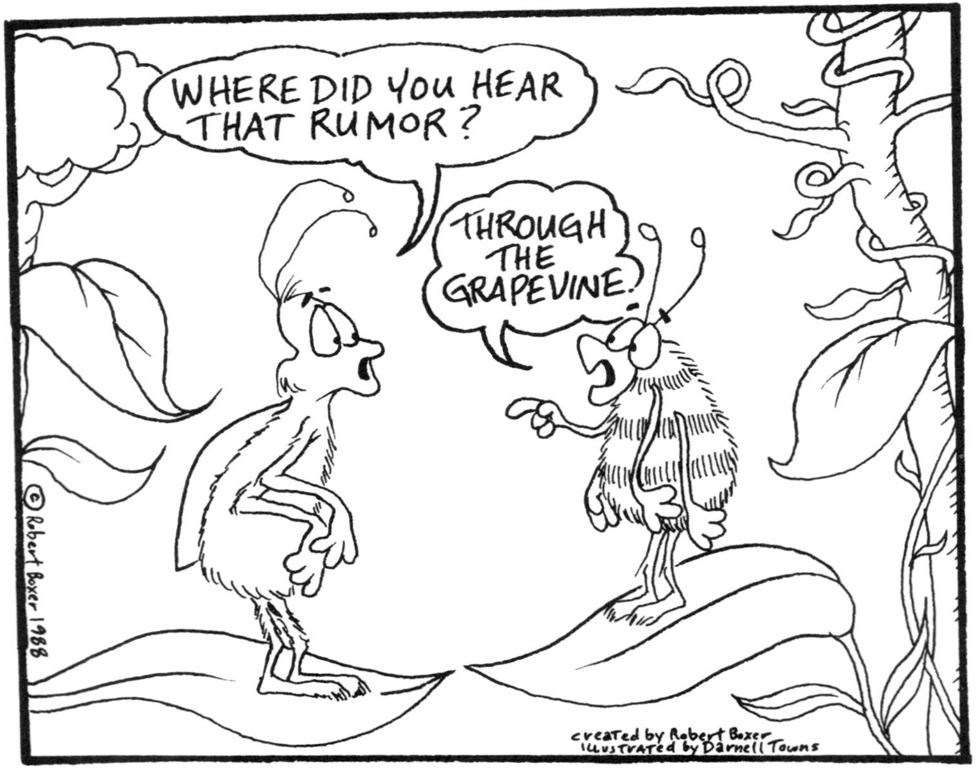
WHERE DID YOU HEAR THAT RUMOR?
THROUGH THE GRAPEVINE.
© Robert Boxer 1988
created by Robert Boxer
illustrated by Darnell Towns

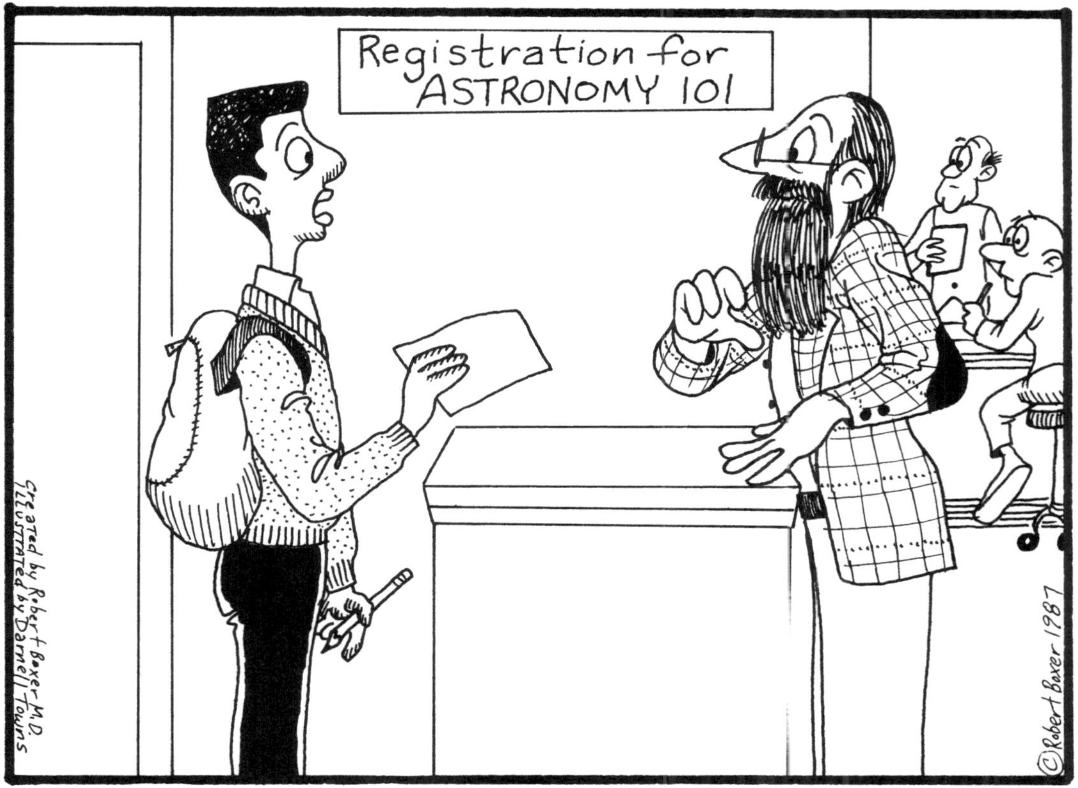
Registration for
ASTRONOMY 101
Created by Robert Boxer M.D.
Illustrated by Darnell Towns
©Robert Boxer 1987

"My Counselor told me to take a light year".

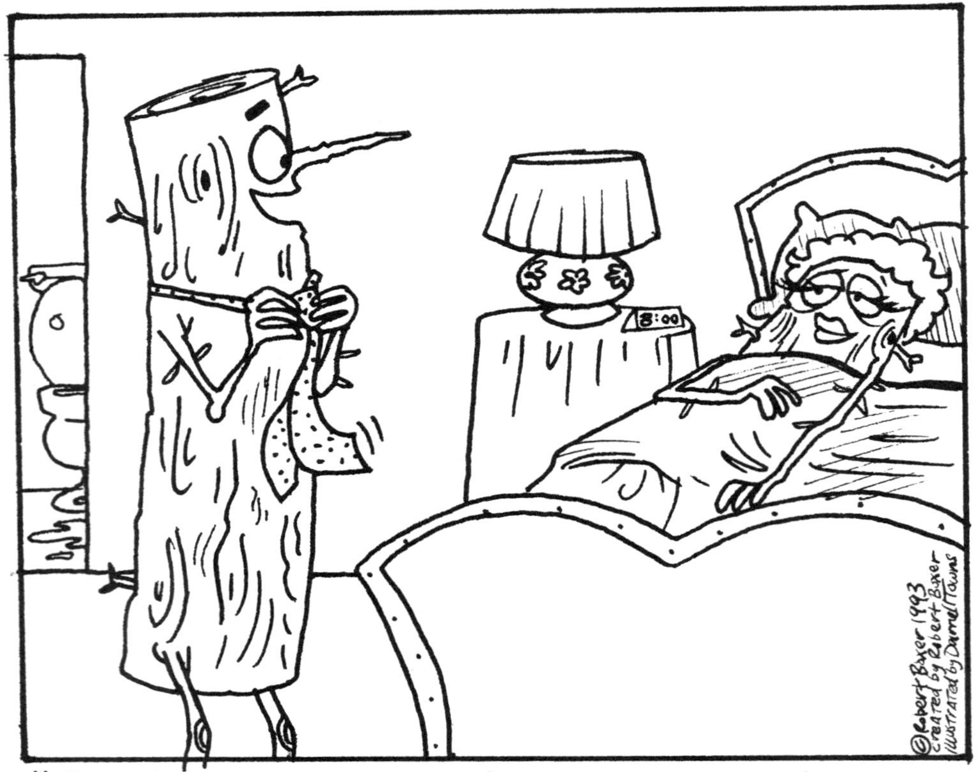
8:00
©Robert Baxer 1993
CREATED by Robert Baxer
ILLUSTRATED by Darrell Towns

"So dear, how did YOU sleep last night."

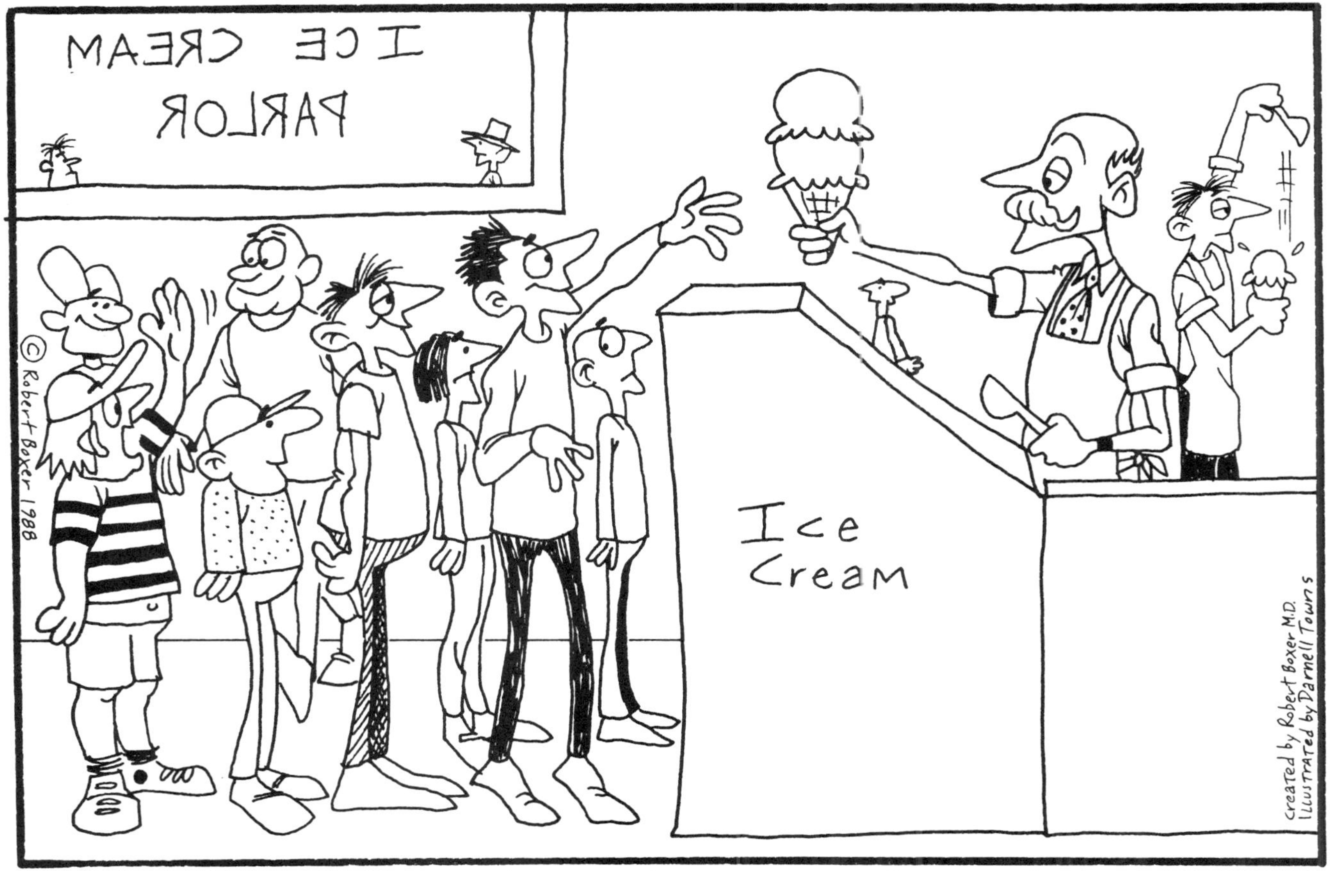
ICE CREAM
PARLOR
© Robert Boxer 1988
Ice
Cream
Created by Robert Boxer M.D.
Illustrated by Darnell Towns

"Let's get into this line. This guy's a State Legislator so we can be sure of getting a Double Dip."

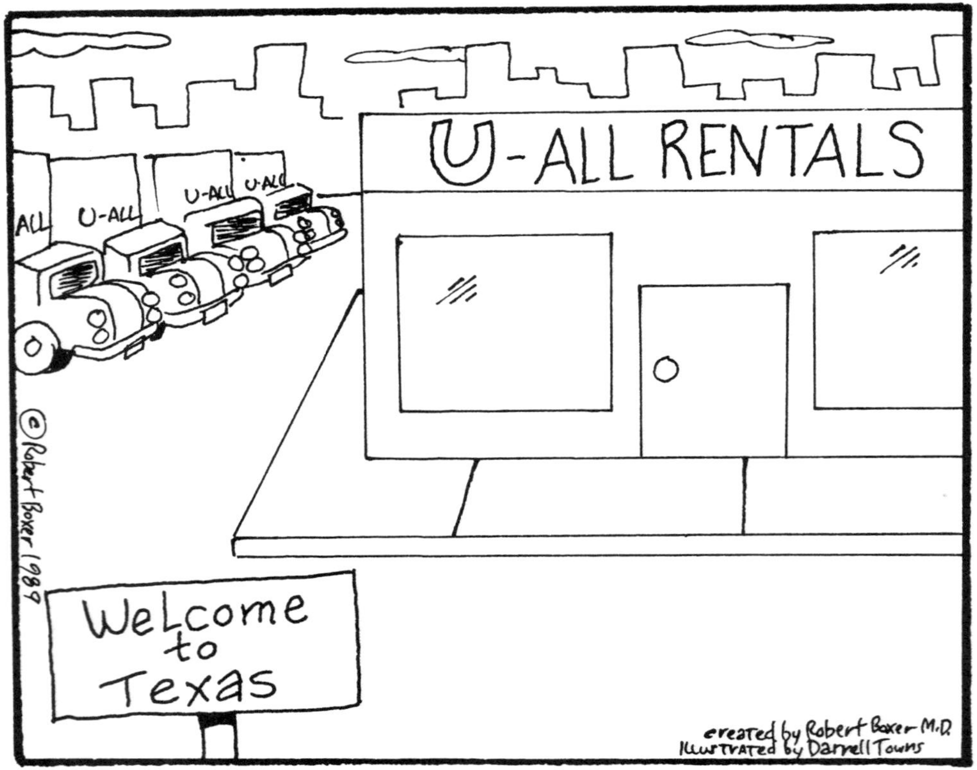
U-ALL RENTALS
U-ALL
U-ALL
U-ALL
ALL
Welcome to Texas
© Robert Boxer 1989
created by Robert Boxer M.D.
Illustrated by Darnell Towns

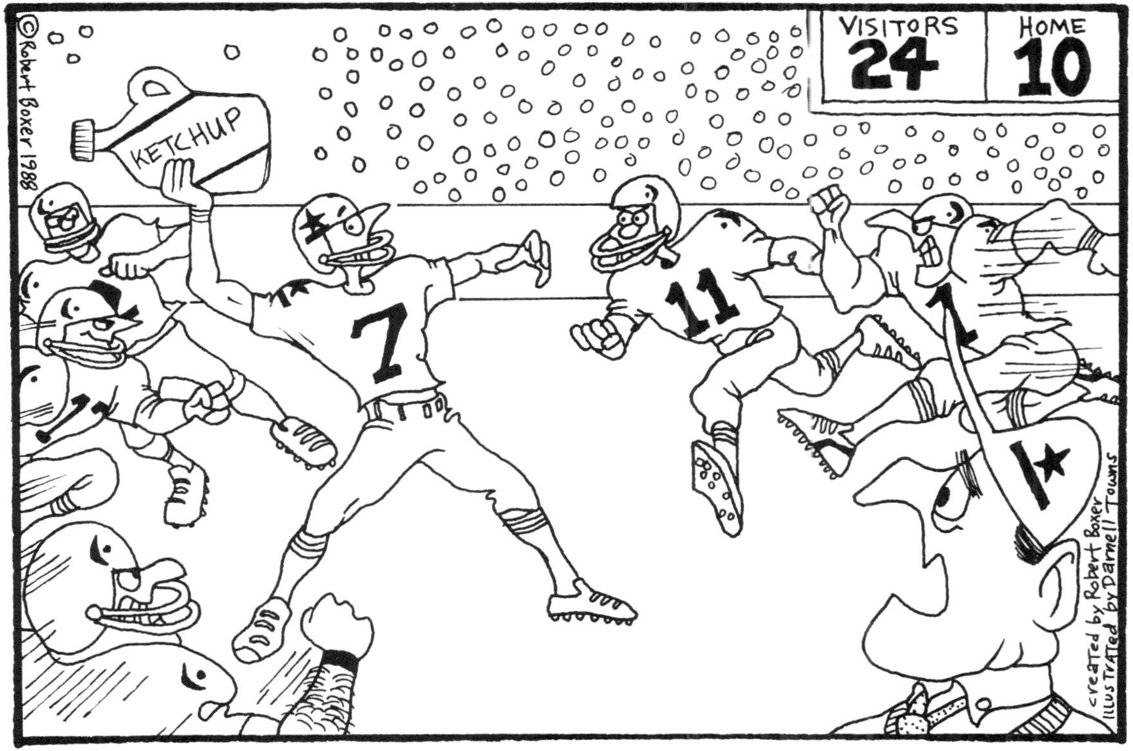

VISITORS
24
HOME
10
KETCHUP
7
11
©Robert Boxer 1988
created by Robert Boxer
ILLUSTRATED by Darnell Towns

"Darn it! Here we are playing
Catch up football again".

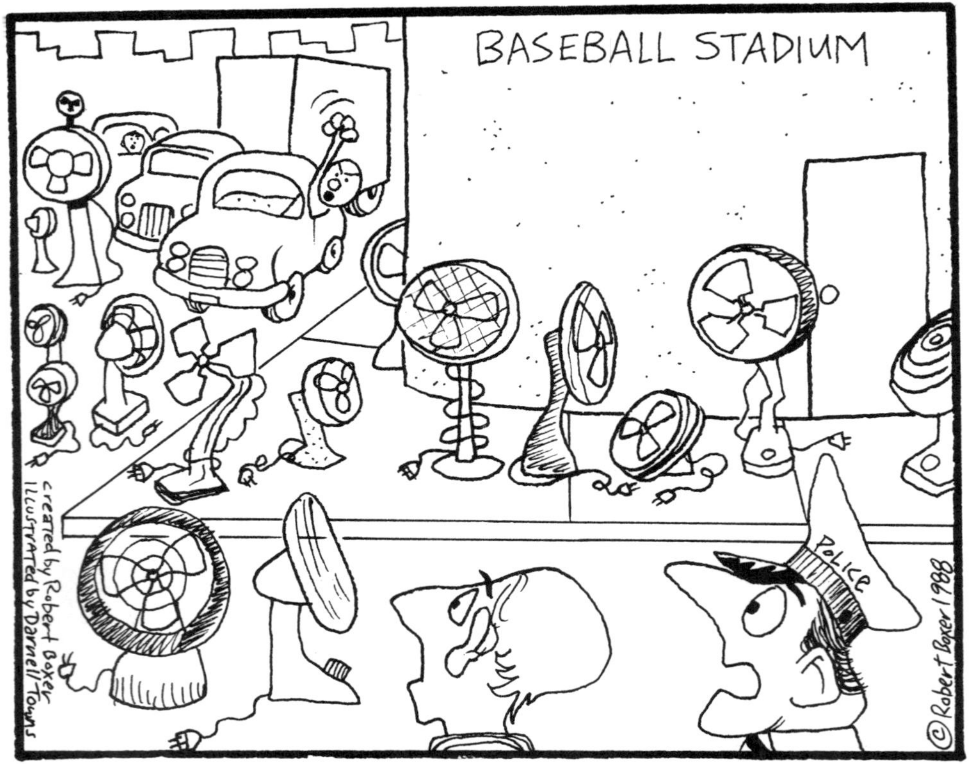
BASEBALL STADIUM
POLICE
created by Robert Boxer
Illustrated by Darnell Towns
© Robert Boxer 1988

"WHAT ARE WE GOING TO DO WITH ALL OF THESE ILLEGALLY PARKED FANS?"

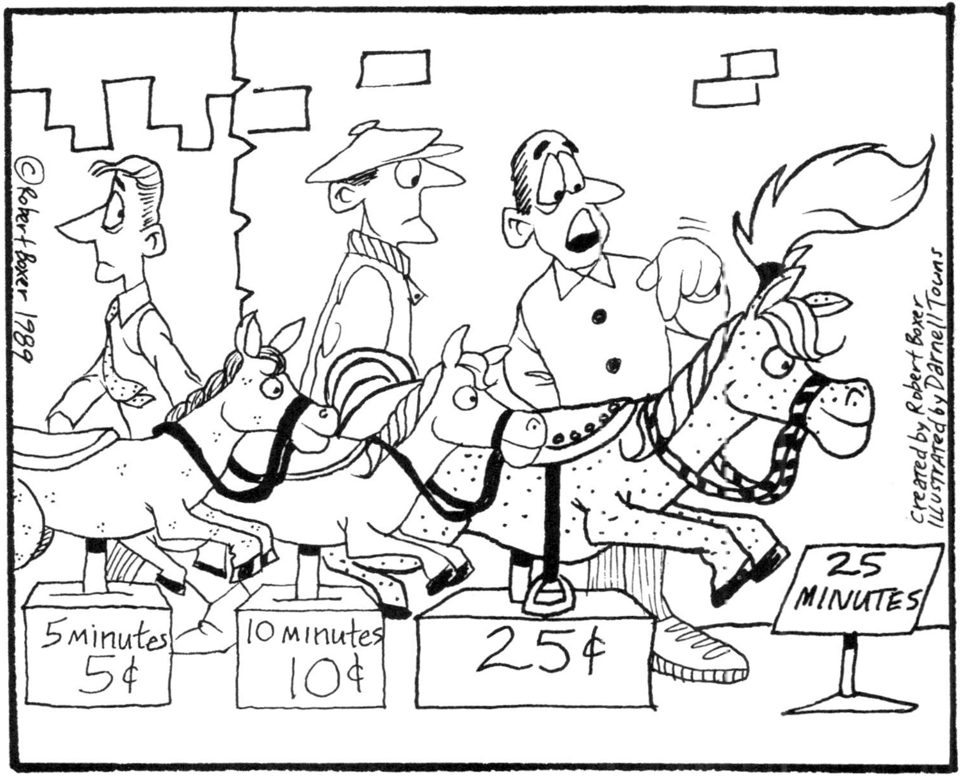
©Robert Boxer 1989
5 minutes
5¢
10 minutes
10¢
25¢
25
MINUTES
Created by Robert Boxer
ILLUSTRATED by Darnell Towns

"This must be a Quarterhorse."

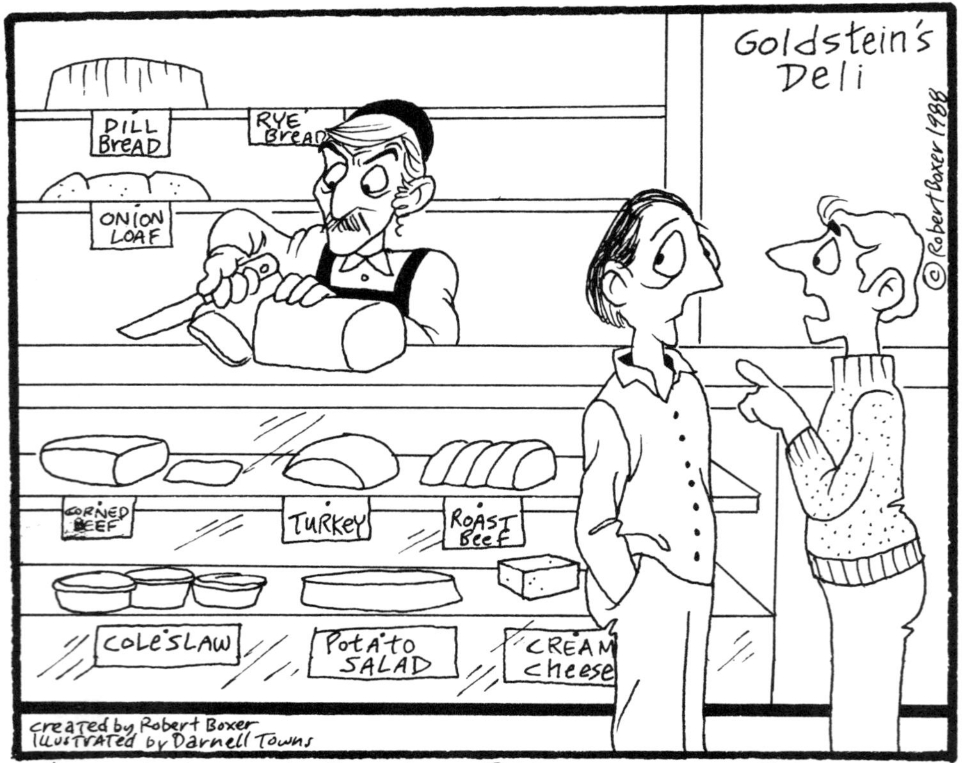
Goldstein's Deli
© Robert Boxer 1988
DILL Bread
RYE Bread
ONION LOAF
CORNED BEEF
TURKEY
ROAST Beef
COLE'SLAW
Potato SALAD
CREAM cheese
created by Robert Boxer
Illustrated by Darnell Towns

"Watch out for his RYE sense of humor."

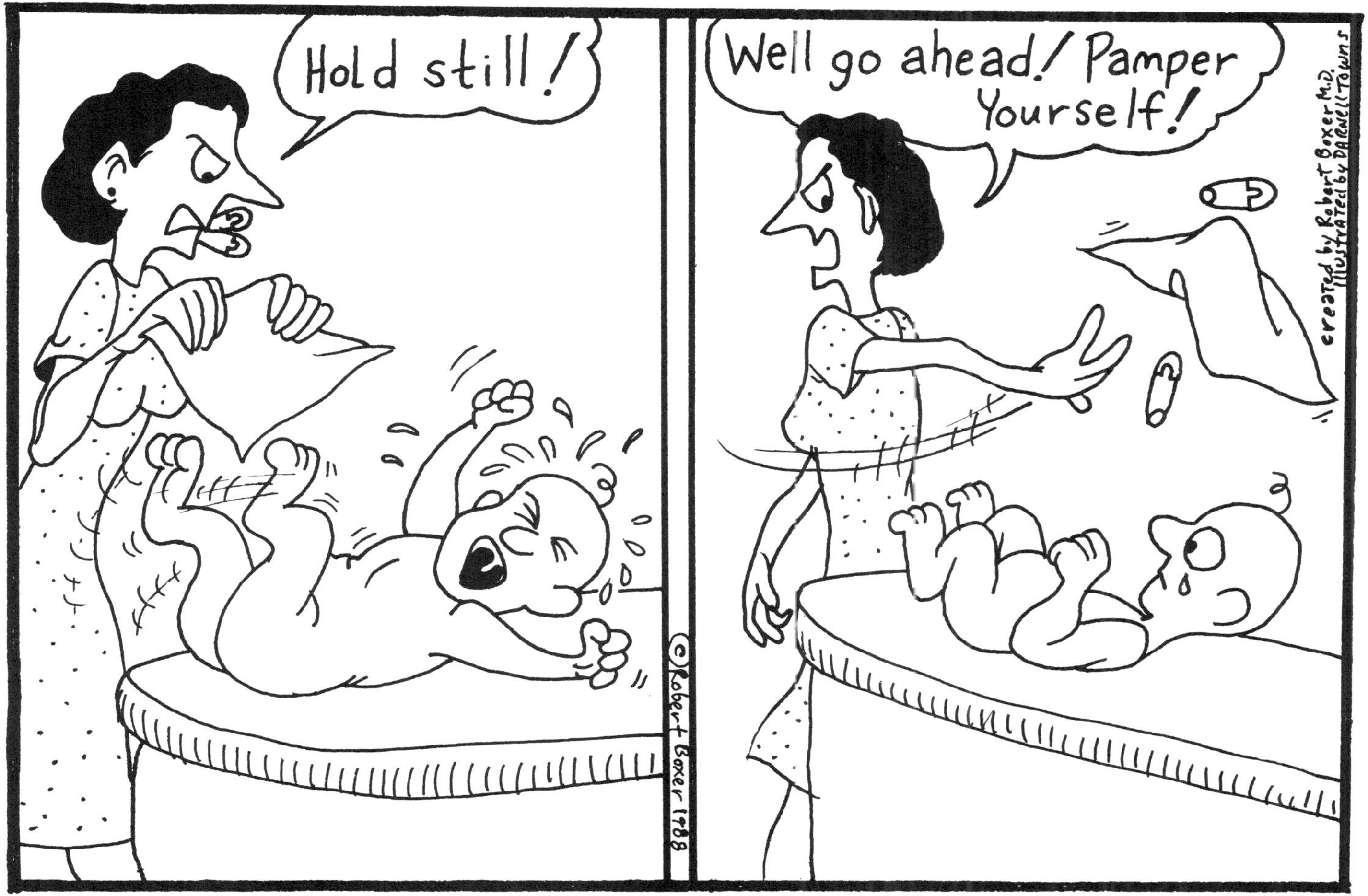
Hold still!
©Robert Boxer 1988
Well go ahead! Pamper Yourself!
created by Robert Boxer M.D.
Illustrated by DARNELL TOWNS

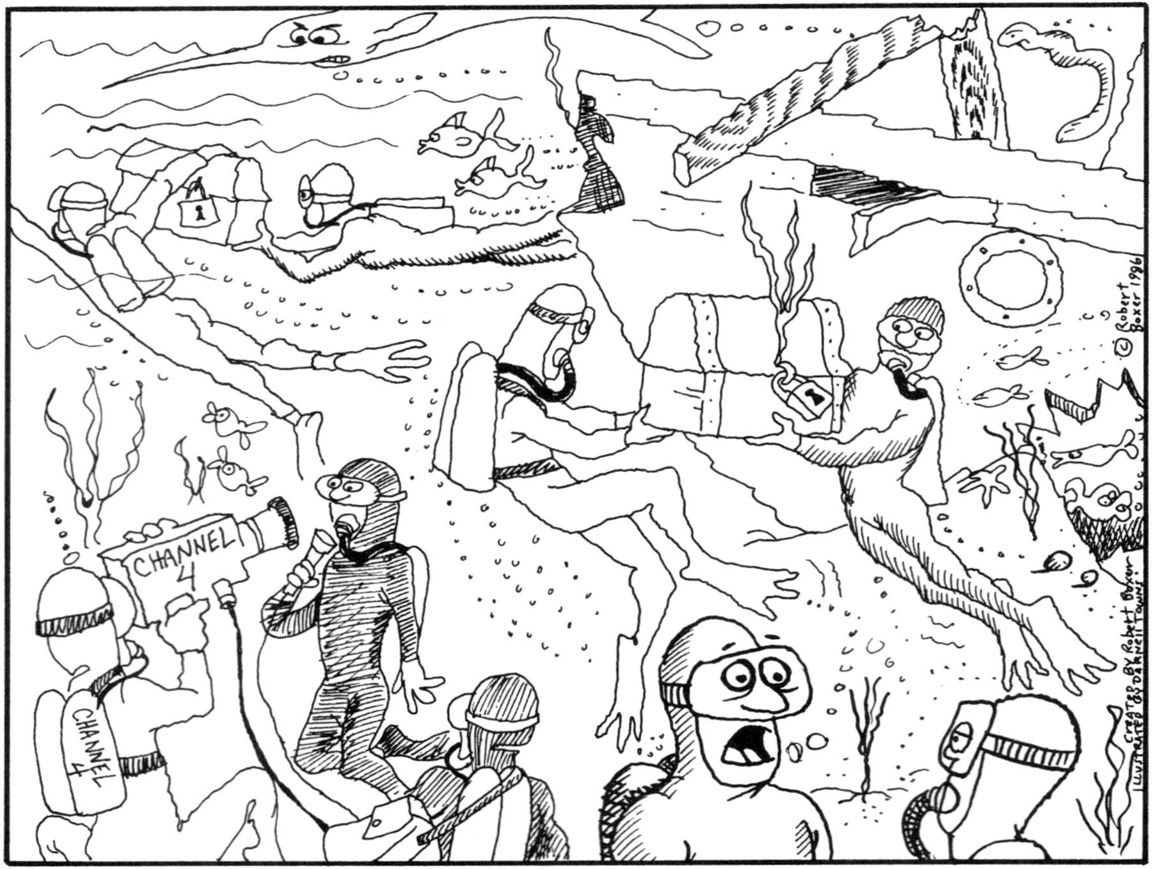
CHANNEL 4
CHANNEL 4
© Robert Boxer 1996
CREATED BY Robert Boxer
ILLUSTRATED BY DARNELL TOWNS

"When I took the job as Anchorman, I had no idea that this was what they meant by reporting the news <u>in-depth</u>."

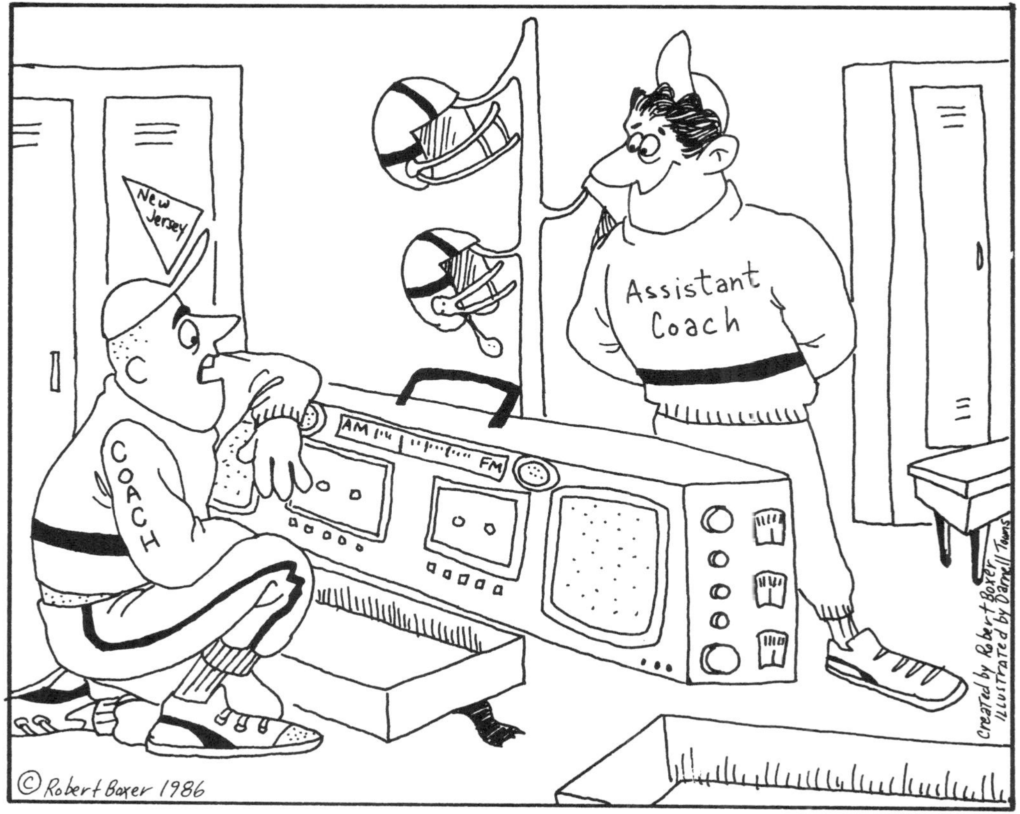
New Jersey
AM
FM
COACH
Assistant Coach
Created by Robert Boxer
Illustrated by Darnell Towns
© Robert Boxer 1986

"Thanks. I did mention I needed a wide receiver".

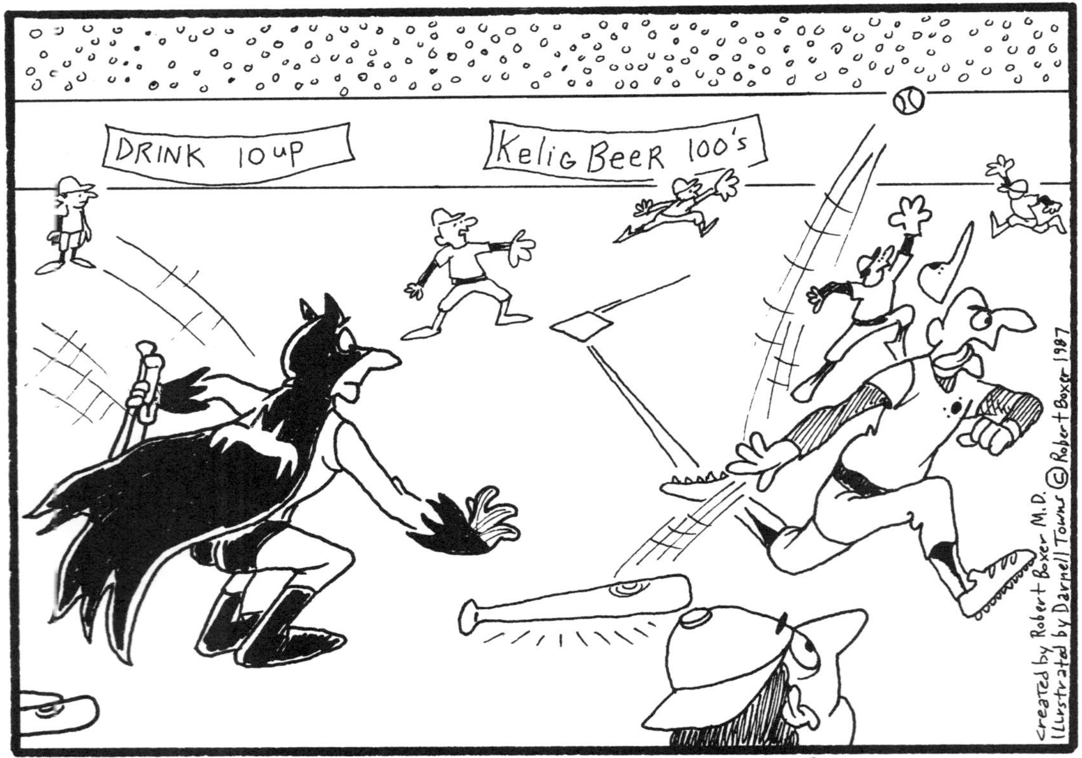
DRINK 10 up
Kelig Beer 100's
created by Robert Boxer M.D.
Illustrated by Darnell Towns © Robert Boxer 1987

"The Batboy is sick, so his Dad is filling in".

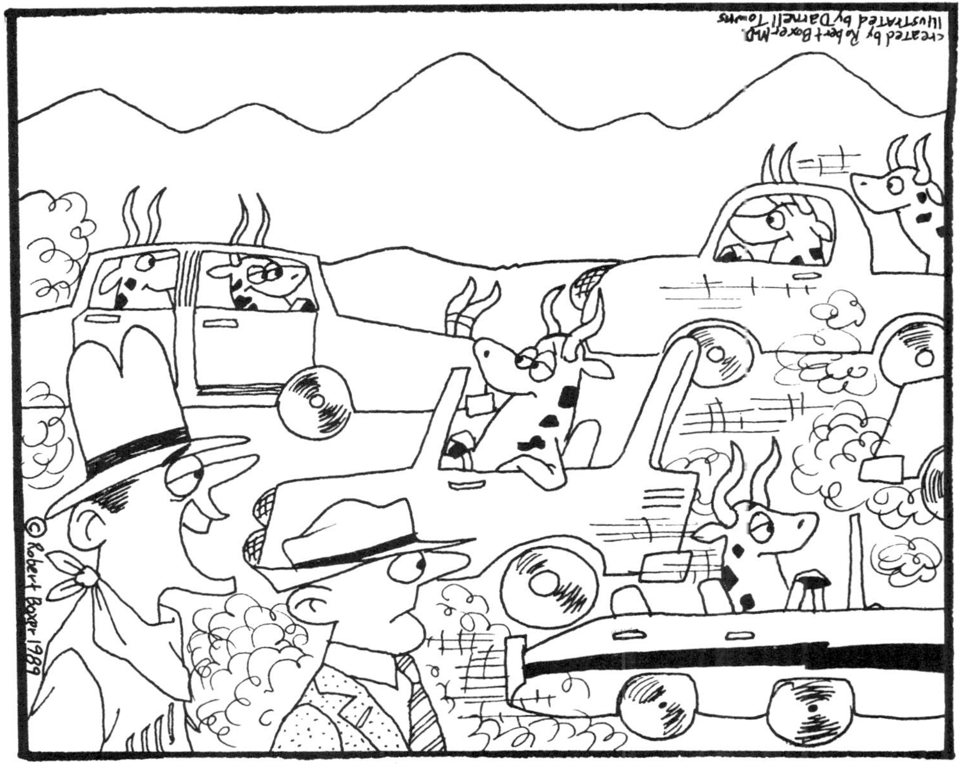
created by Robert Boxer,MD.
Illustrated by Darnell Towns
© Robert Boxer 1989

"I Know that you've always wanted to see a cattle drive.

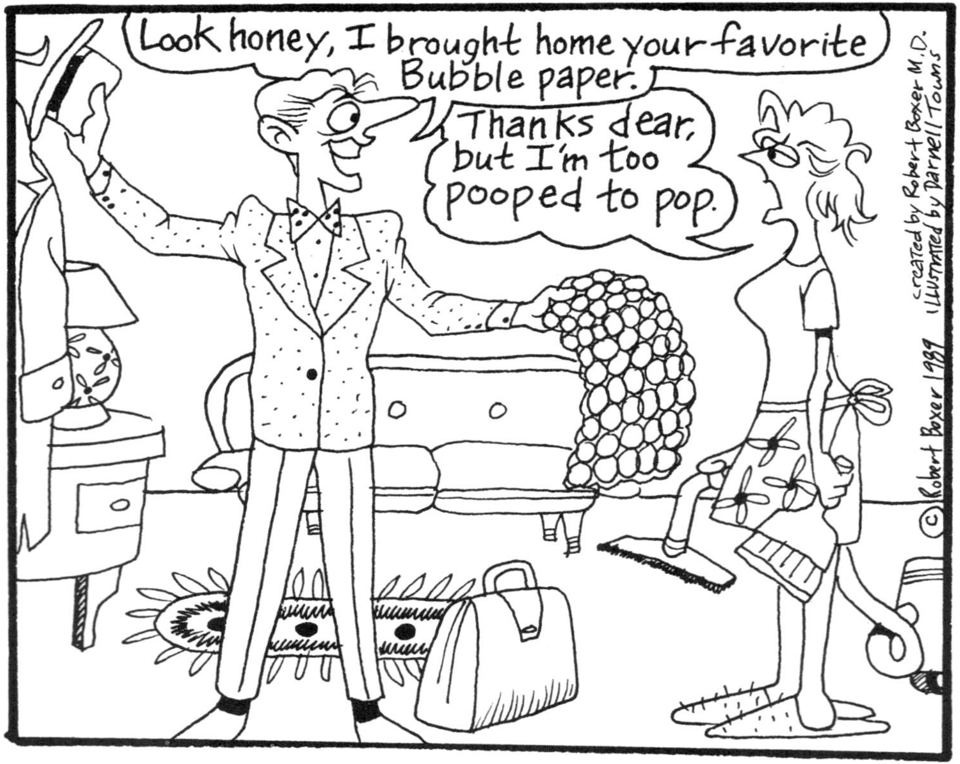
Look honey, I brought home your favorite Bubble paper.
Thanks dear, but I'm too pooped to pop.
created by Robert Boxer M.D.
ILLUSTRATED by Darnell Towns
© Robert Boxer 1989

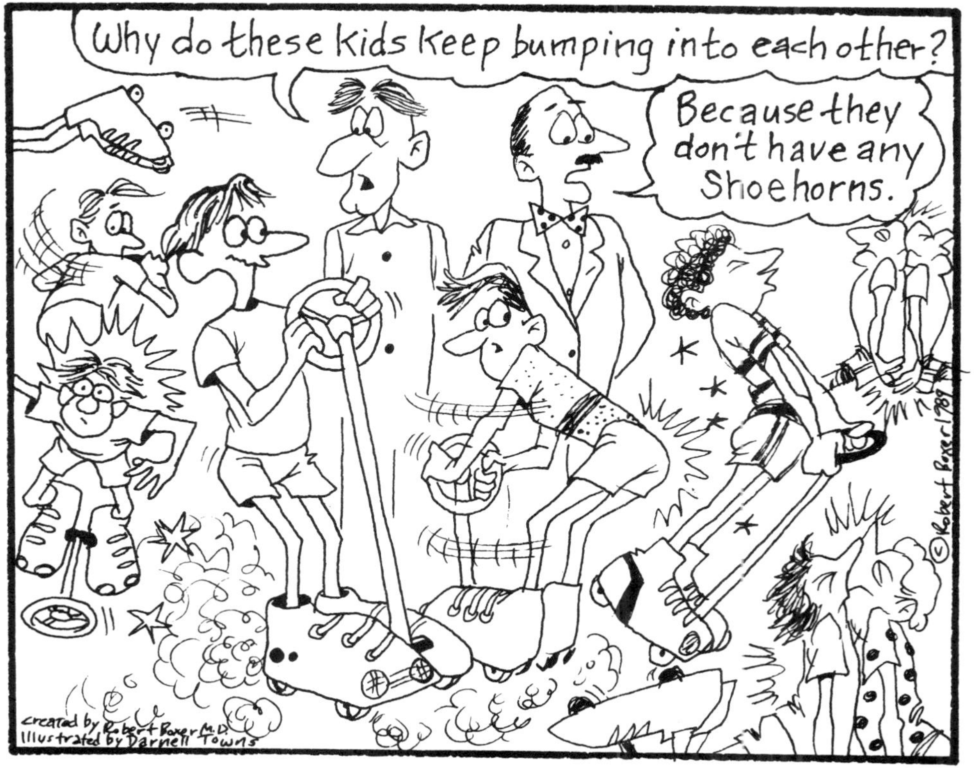
Why do these kids keep bumping into each other?
Because they don't have any Shoehorns.
© Robert Boxer 1989
created by Robert Boxer M.D.
Illustrated by Darnell Towns

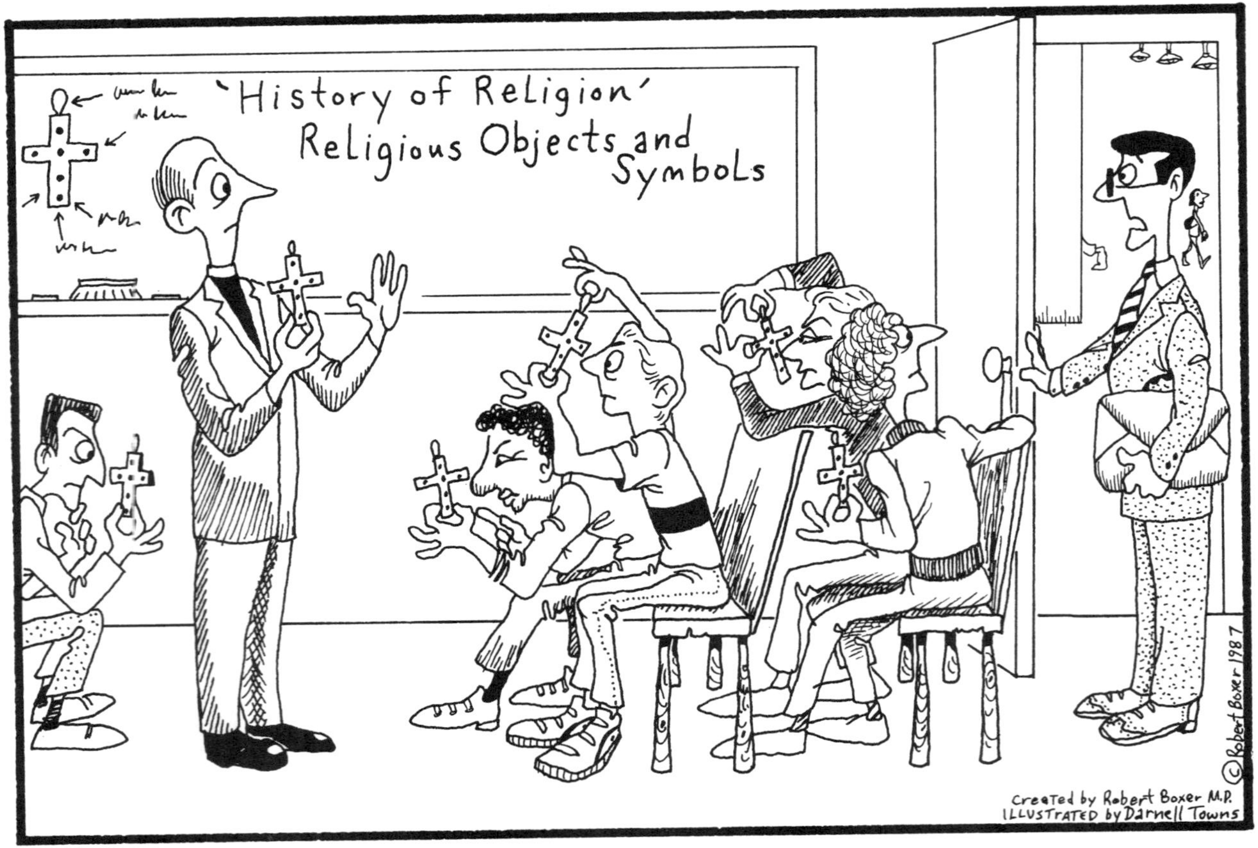
'History of Religion'
Religious Objects and Symbols
© Robert Boxer 1987
Created by Robert Boxer M.D.
ILLUSTRATED by Darnell Towns

'Pardon me. I thought this class was part of the Law School. The Outside sign reads 'Cross Examination Today'.

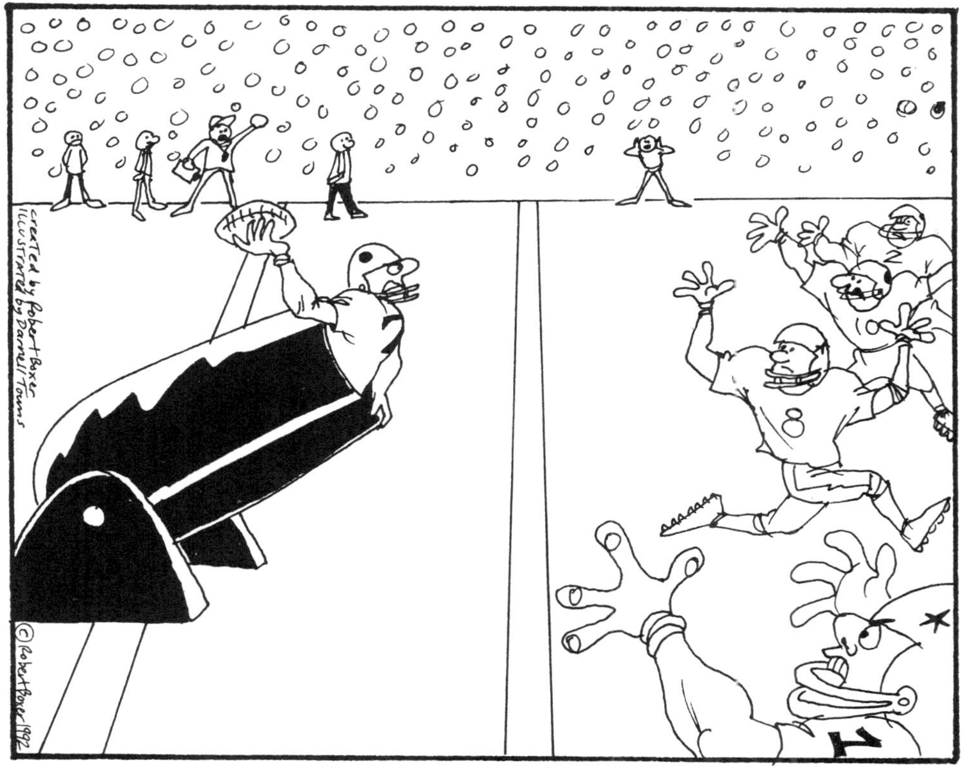
created by Robert Baxer
illustrated by Darrell Toms
© Robert Baxer 1992

ANNOUNCER: "And now the Quarterback is throwing out of the Gun!"

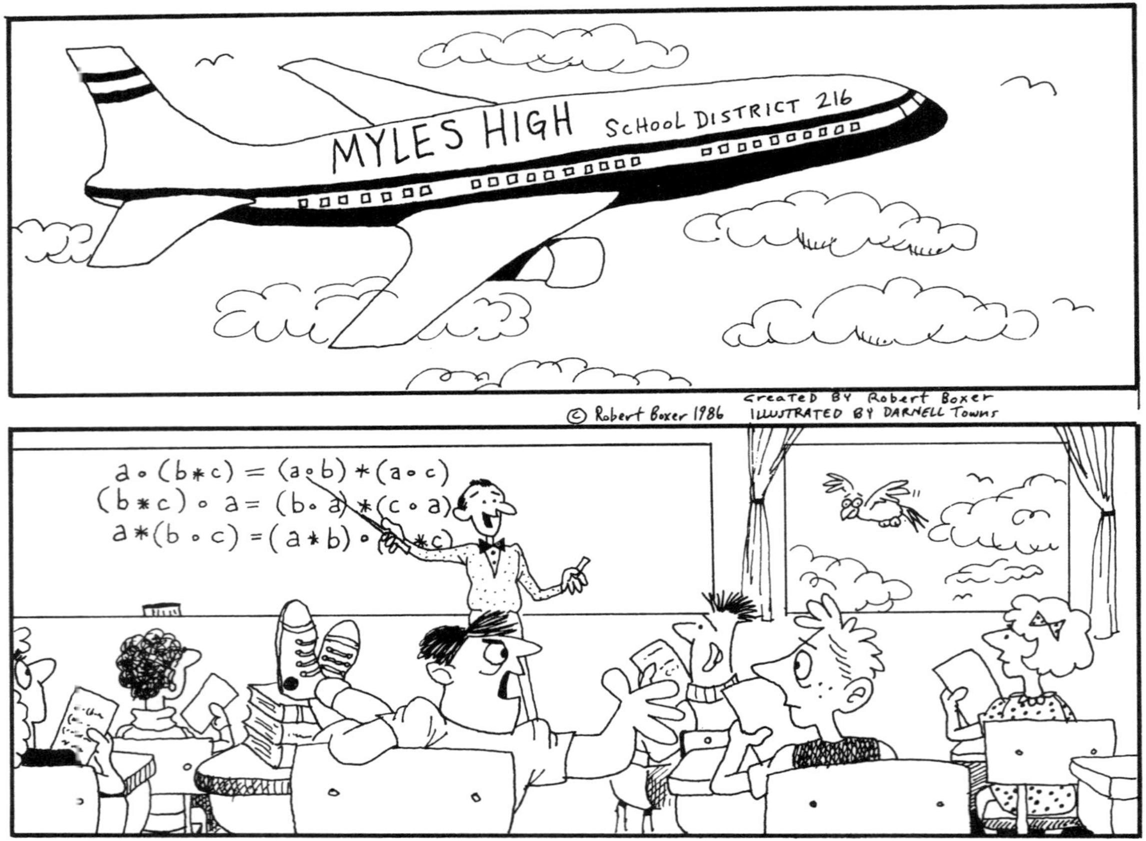
MYLES HIGH
SCHOOL DISTRICT 216
© Robert Boxer 1986
CREATED BY Robert Boxer
ILLUSTRATED BY DARNELL Towns
a ∘ (b ∗ c) = (a ∘ b) ∗ (a ∘ c)
(b ∗ c) ∘ a = (b ∘ a) ∗ (c ∘ a)
a ∗ (b ∘ c) = (a ∗ b) ∘

"Ever since they got the funds and the OK to hold classes up here, they have reduced the previously high dropout rate to zero".

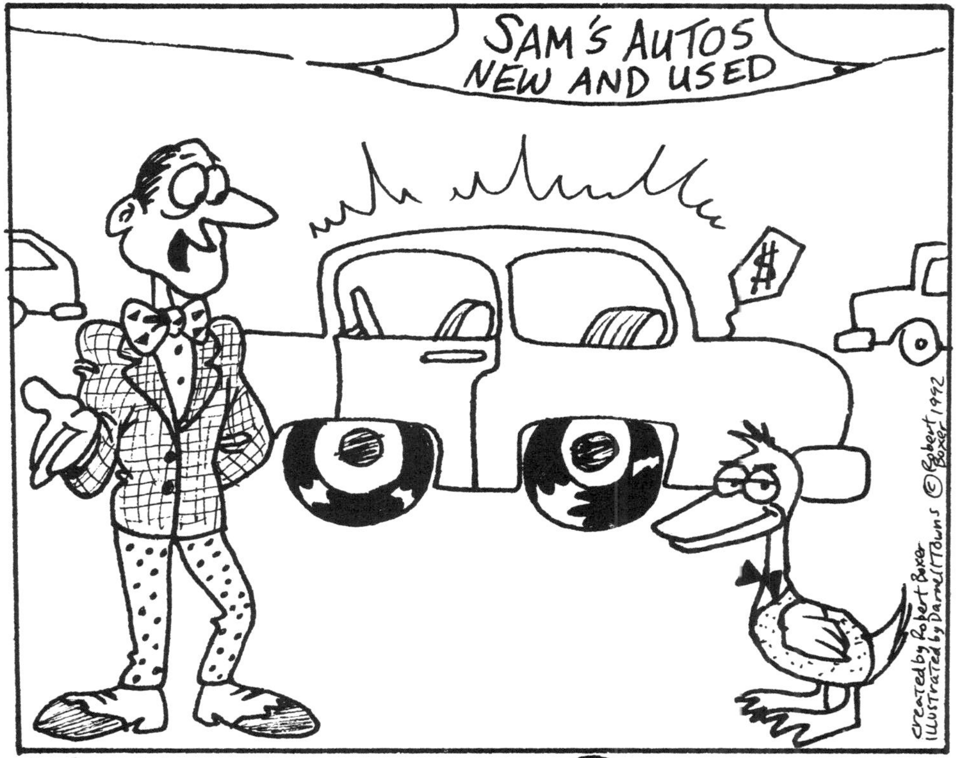
SAM'S AUTOS
NEW AND USED
$
©Robert Boxer 1992
created by Robert Boxer
illustrated by Darnell Towns

"Would you like to make a **DOWN** payment?"

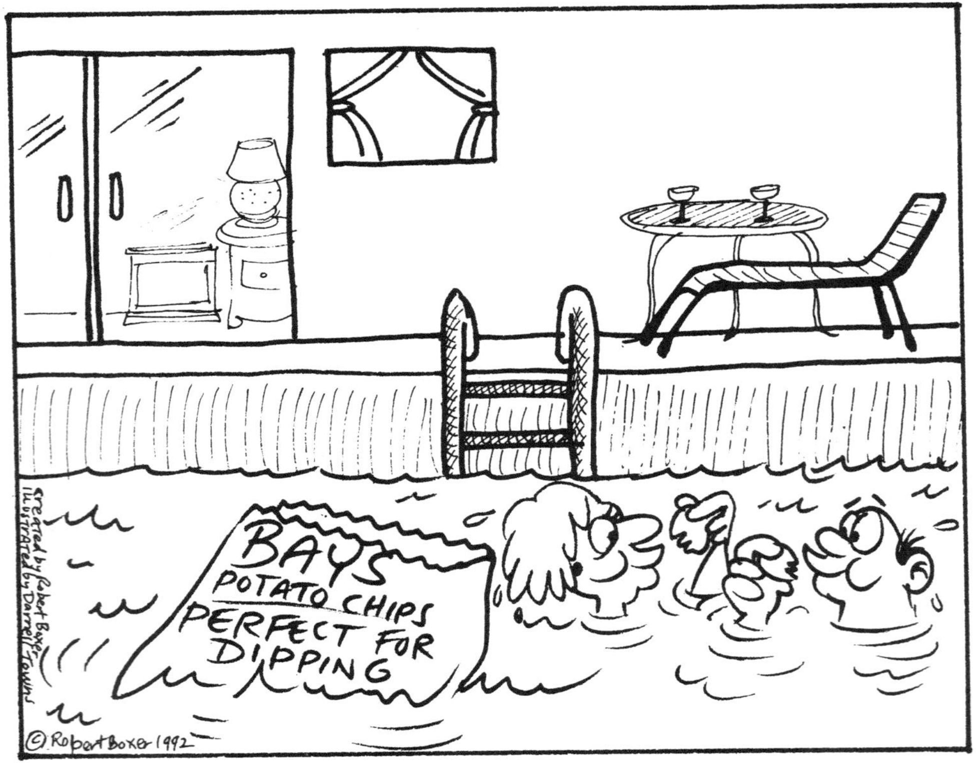
BAYS
POTATO CHIPS
PERFECT FOR DIPPING
created by Robert Boxer
illustrated by Darnell Towns
© Robert Boxer 1992

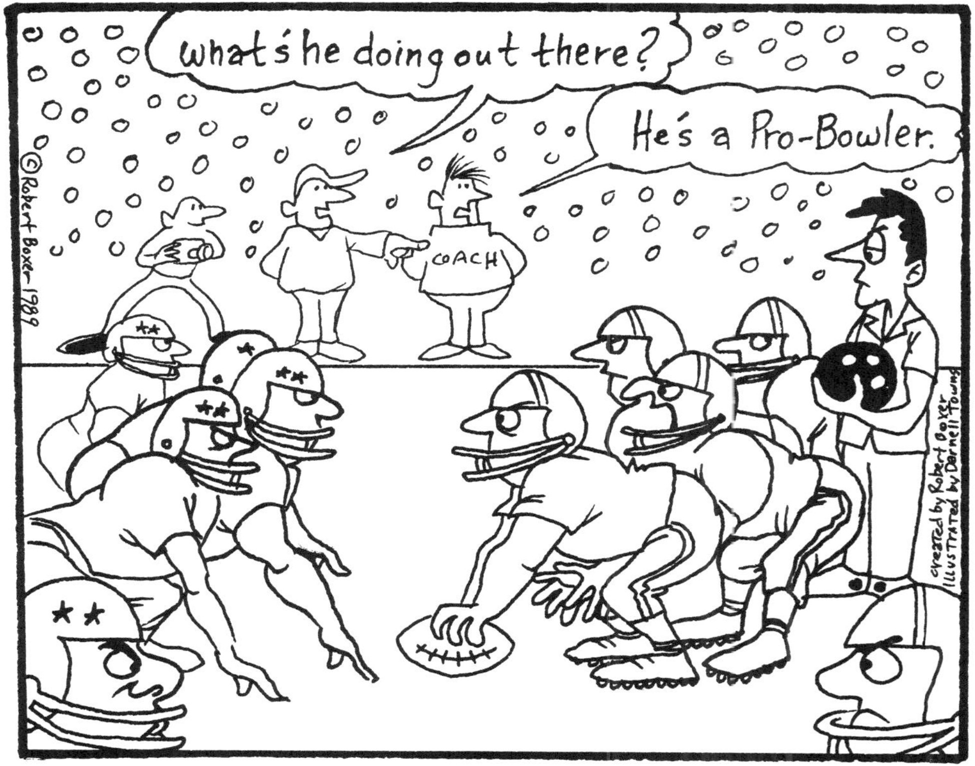
what's he doing out there?
He's a Pro-Bowler.
COACH
© Robert Boxer 1989
created by Robert Boxer
ILLUSTRATED by Darnell Towns

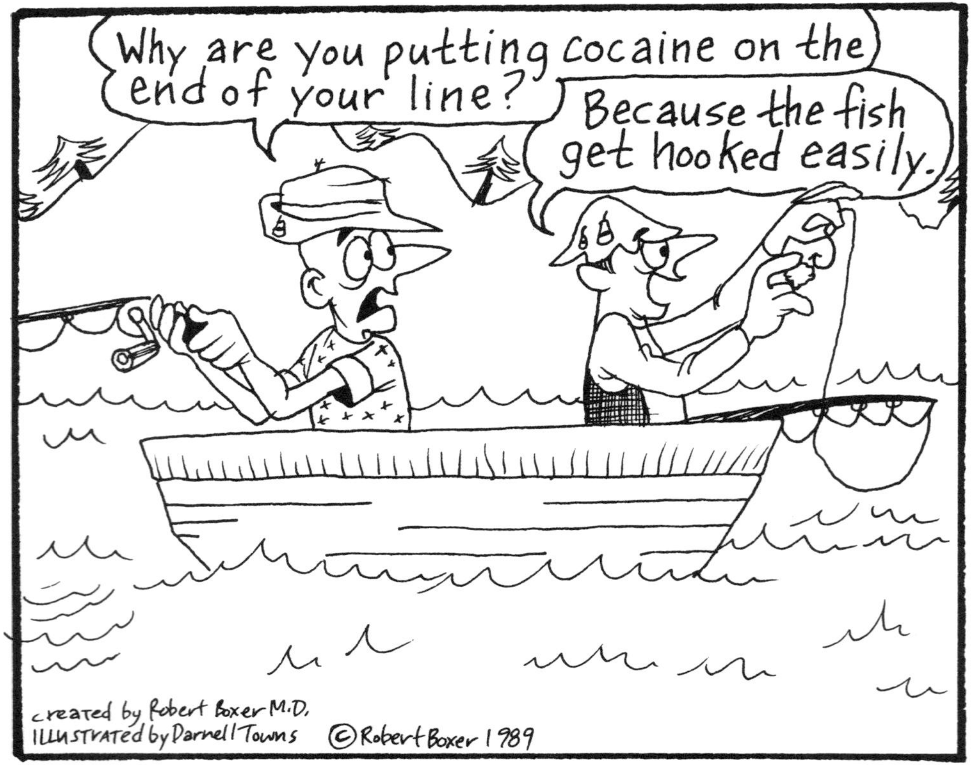
Why are you putting cocaine on the end of your line?
Because the fish get hooked easily.
created by Robert Boxer M.D.
ILLUSTRATED by Darnell Towns
©Robert Boxer 1989

©Robert Boxer 1990
BIG JOHN'S EXTERMINATORS
So what makes you think you've got Carpenter Ants?"
JOHN
Created by Robert Boxer
Illustrated by Darrell Town

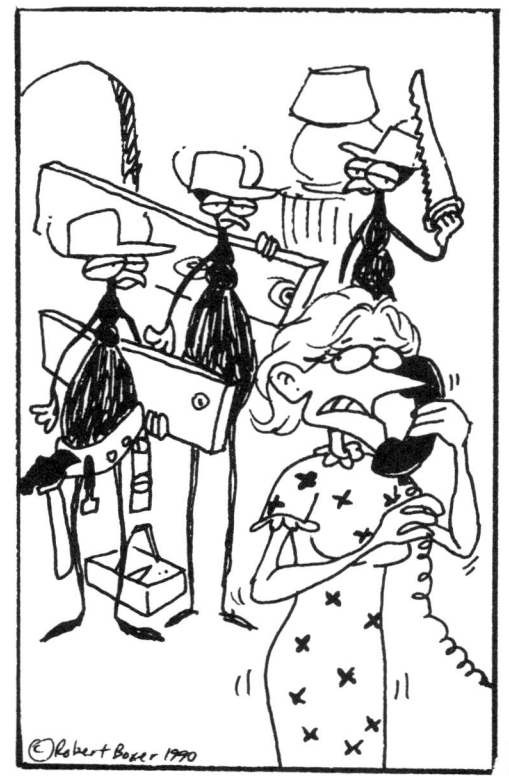

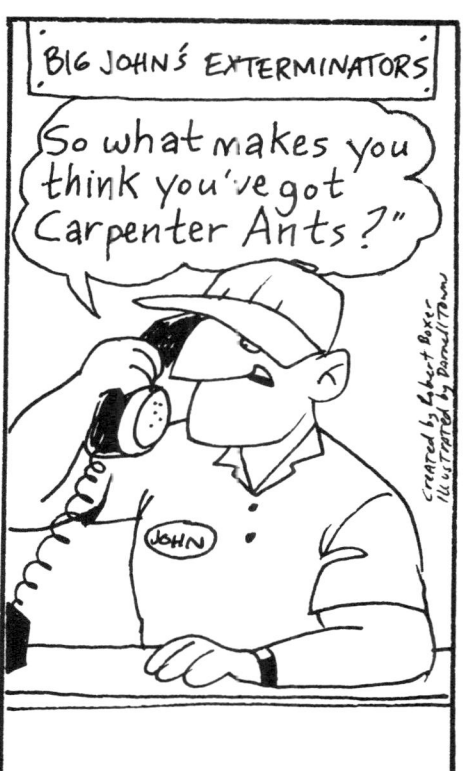

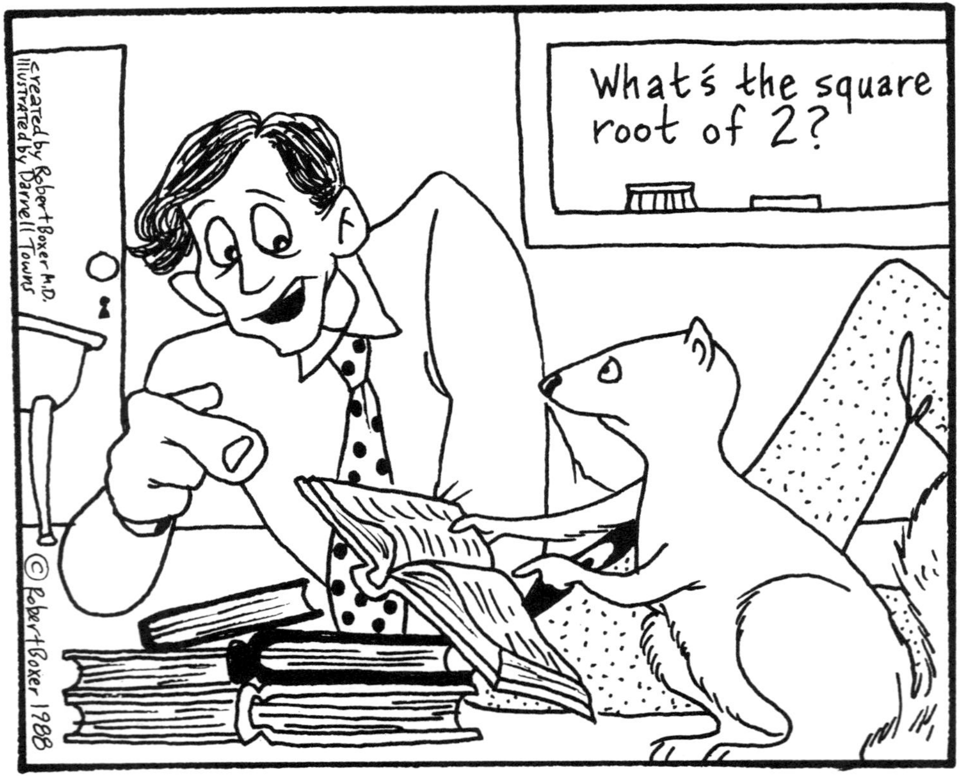
What's the square root of 2?
created by Robert Boxer M.D.
Illustrated by Darnell Towns
© Robert Boxer 1988

"I can't help you with this problem. You're going to have to <u>ferret</u> this one out yourself."

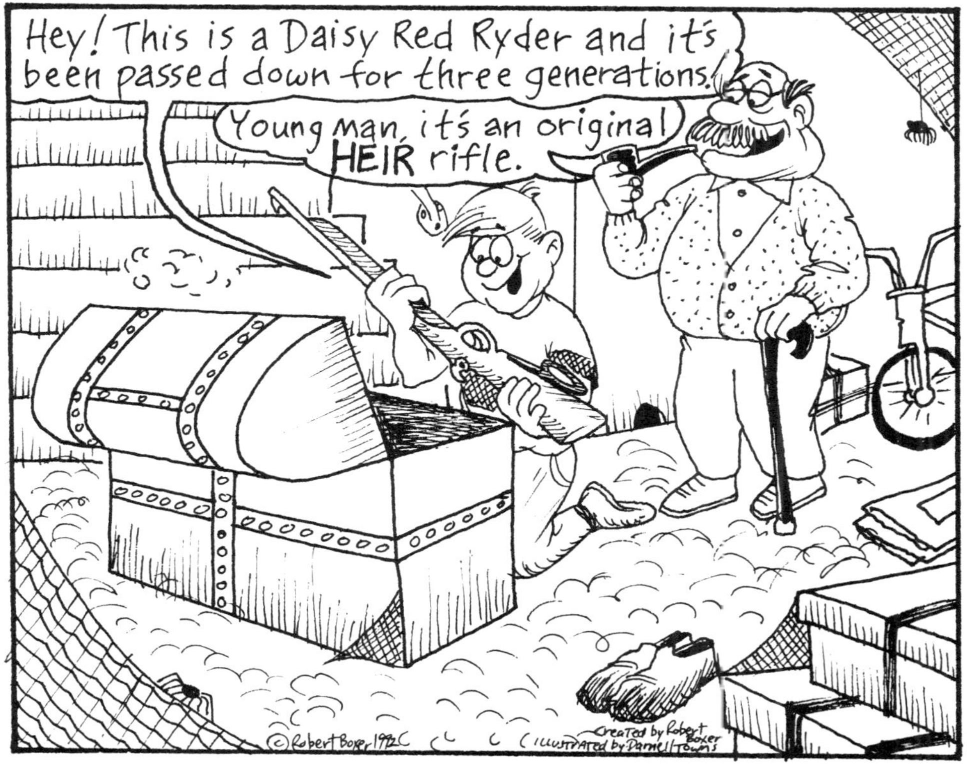
Hey! This is a Daisy Red Ryder and it's been passed down for three generations!
Young man, it's an original HEIR rifle.
©Robert Boxer, 1992
Created by Robert Boxer
Illustrated by Darnell Towns

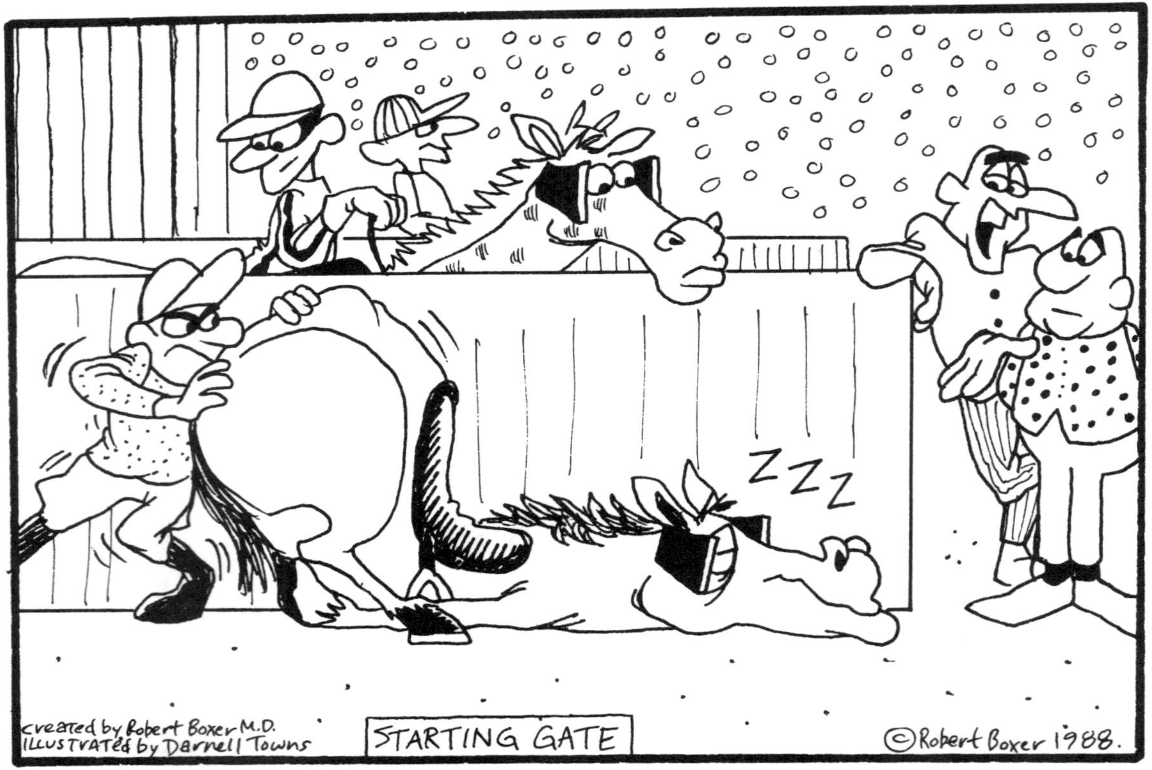
ZZZ
created by Robert Boxer M.D.
ILLUSTRATED by Darnell Towns
STARTING GATE
©Robert Boxer 1988.

"CAN YOU TELL WHO'S THE SLEEPER IN THIS RACE."

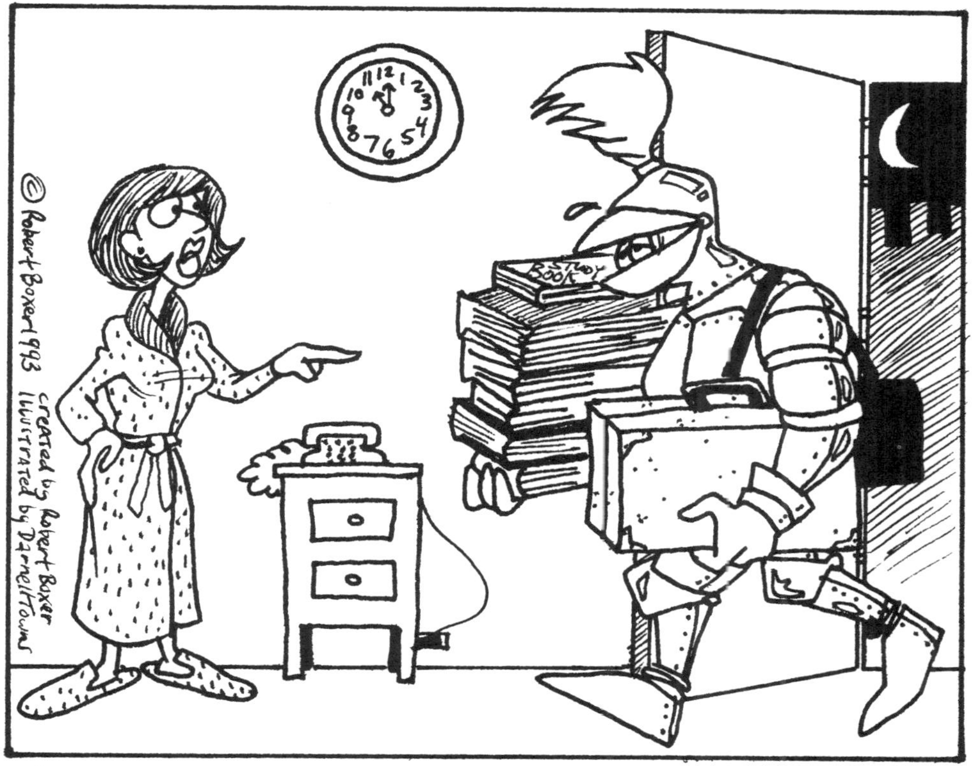
© Robert Boxer 1993
created by Robert Boxer
illustrated by Darnell Towns
STUDY BOOK

"Honey, maybe you're pushing it too hard by working full-time and going to Knight school."

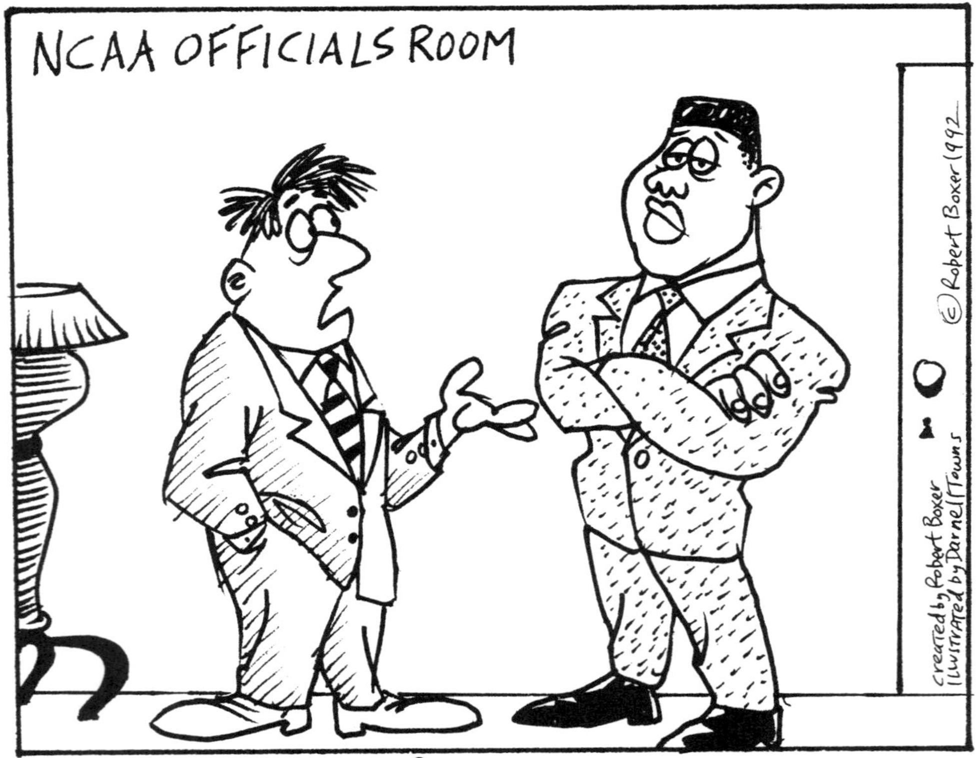
NCAA OFFICIALS ROOM
© Robert Boxer 1992
Created by Robert Boxer
Illustrated by Darnell Towns

"How about a new Bowl game and we'll call it the 'FISH BOWL'. The colleges won't get paid but they'll play just for the HALIBUT."

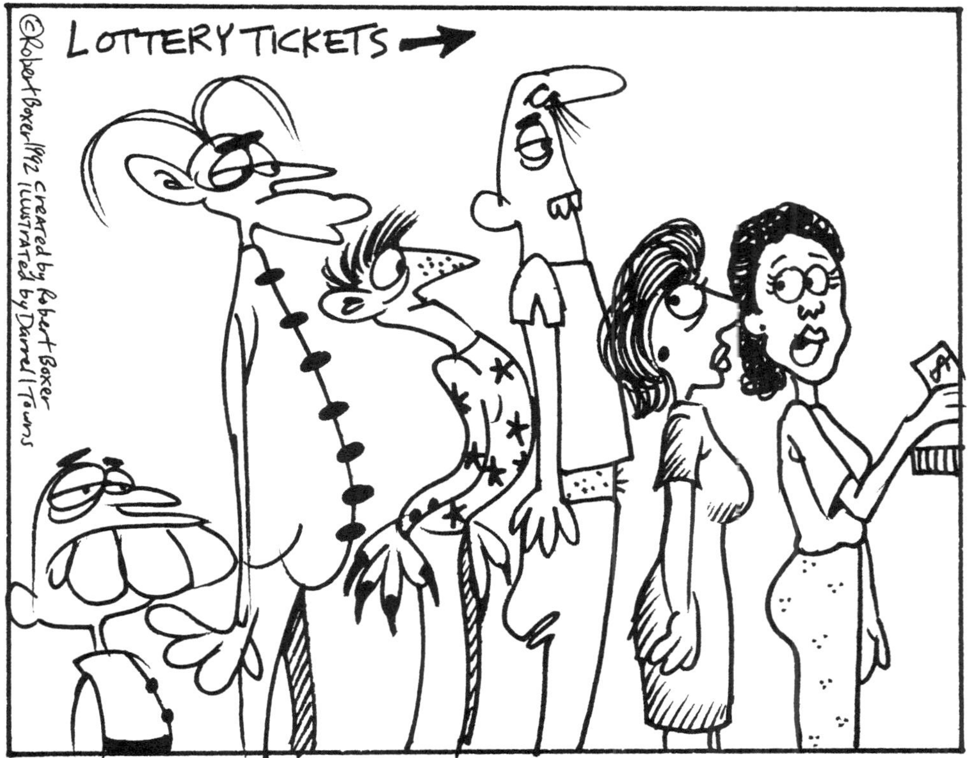
LOTTERY TICKETS →
©Robert Boxer 1992 Created by Robert Boxer
Illustrated by Darrell Towns

"You Know, I'm used to winning, even against all ODDS."

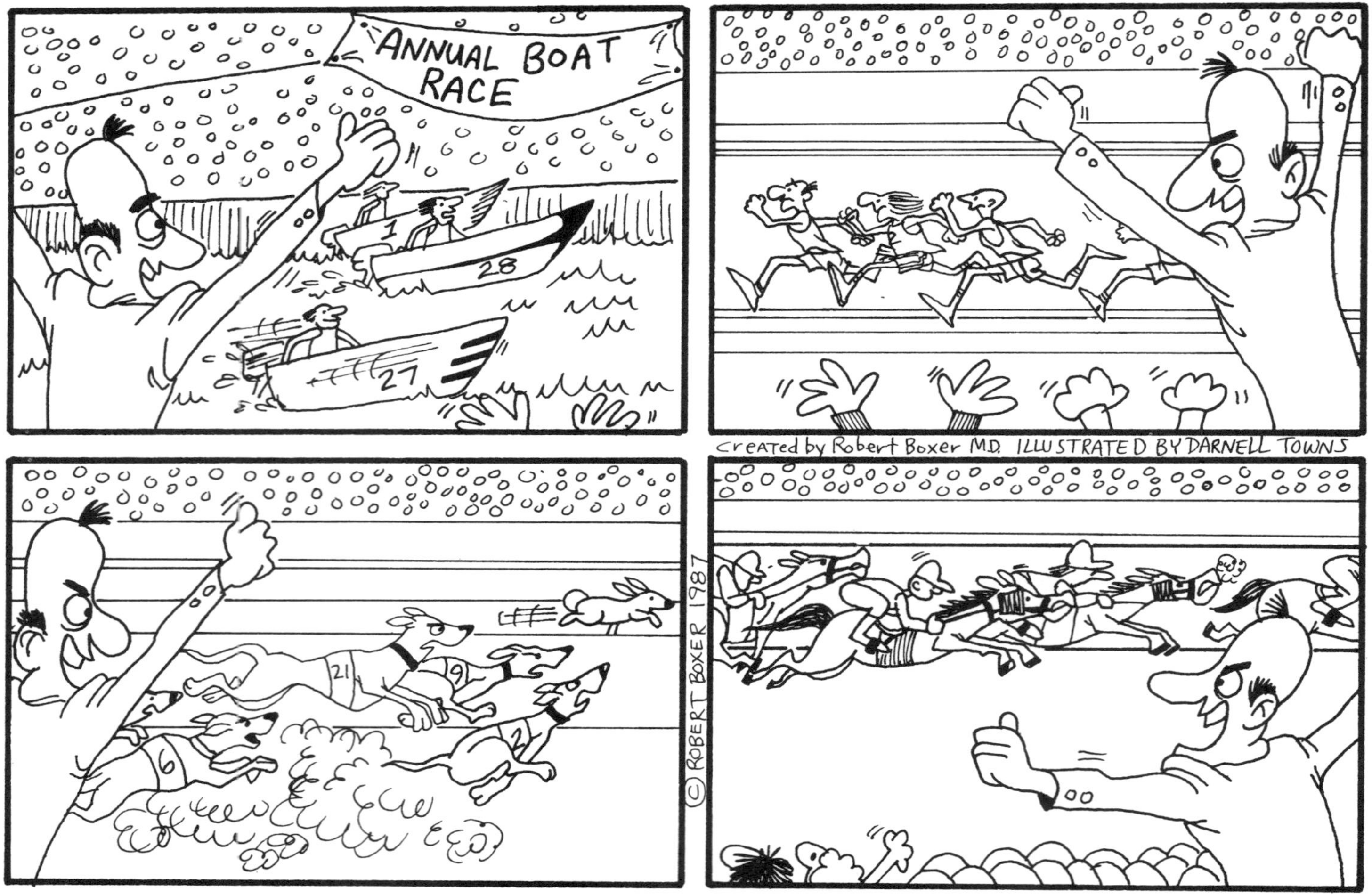
ANNUAL BOAT RACE
1
28
27
created by Robert Boxer M.D. ILLUSTRATED BY DARNELL TOWNS
© ROBERT BOXER 1987
21
9
6
2

RACIST

STATE U.
KETCHUP
?
© Robert Boxer 1992
created by Robert Boxer
illustrated by Darrell Towns

"Coach, said this weekend, be sure to get some CATCH UP sleep."

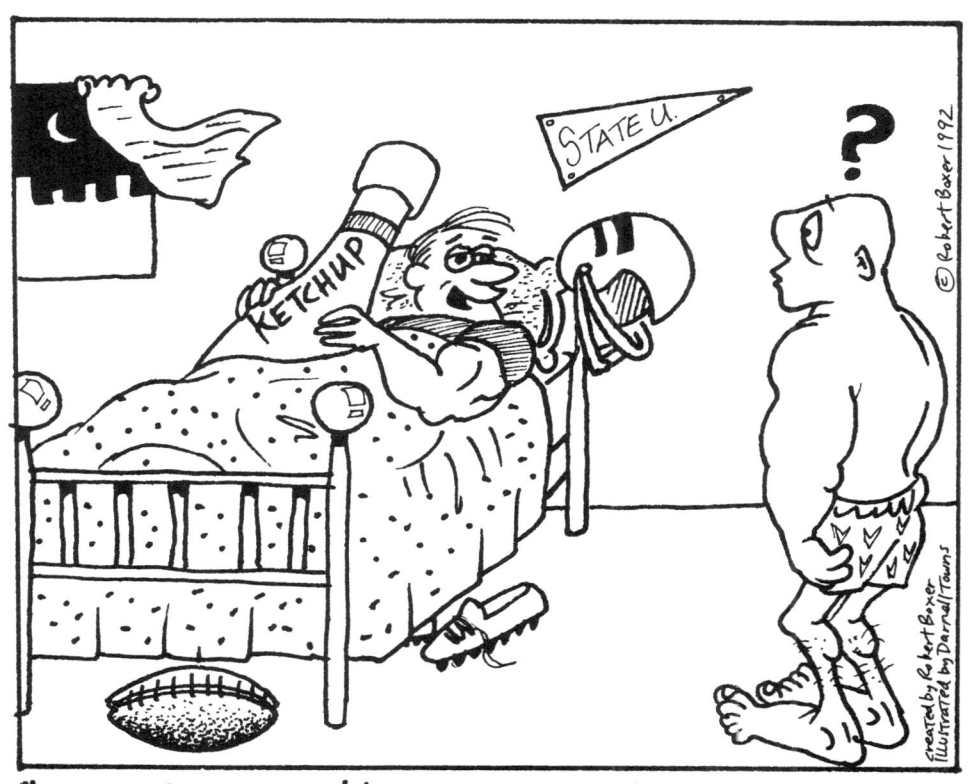

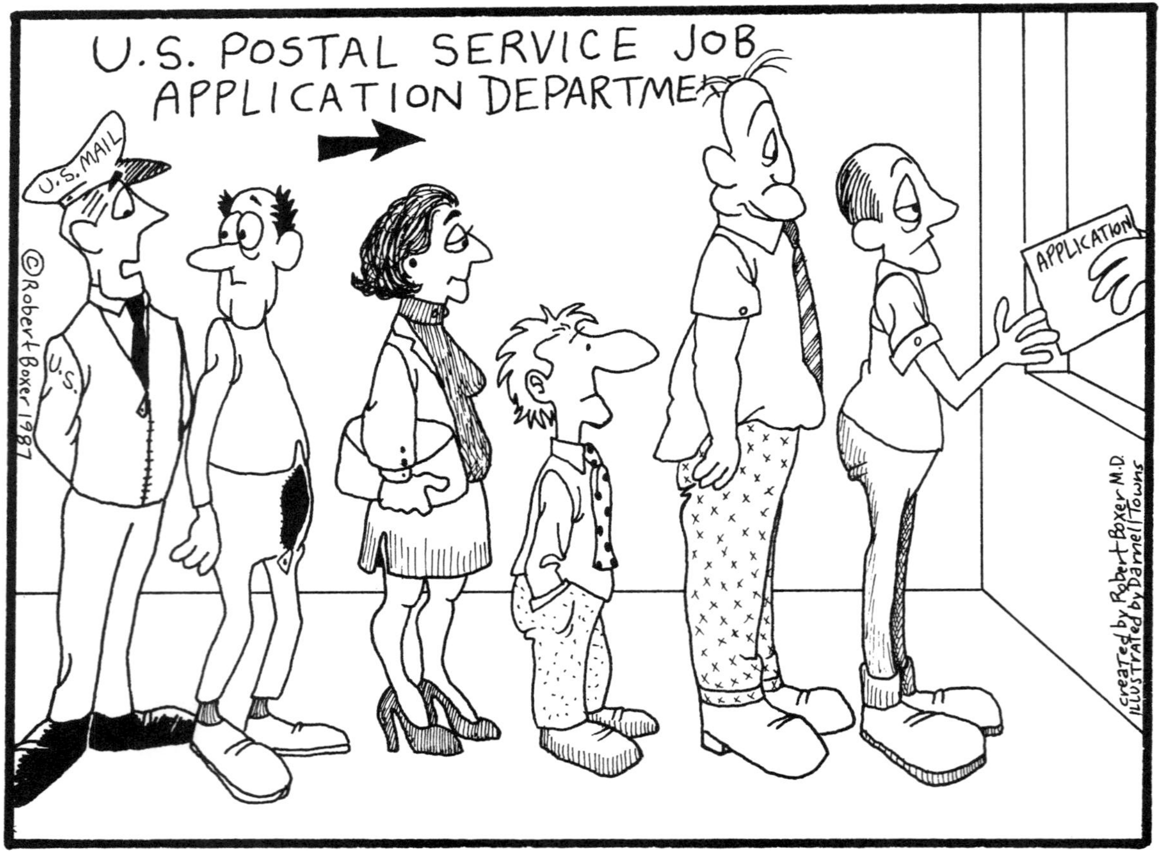
U.S. POSTAL SERVICE JOB
APPLICATION DEPARTMENT
U.S. MAIL
U.S.
APPLICATION
©Robert Boxer 1987
created by Robert Boxer M.D.
ILLUSTRATED by Darnell Towns

"You apparently don't know the ZIP codes well enough to apply for the job."

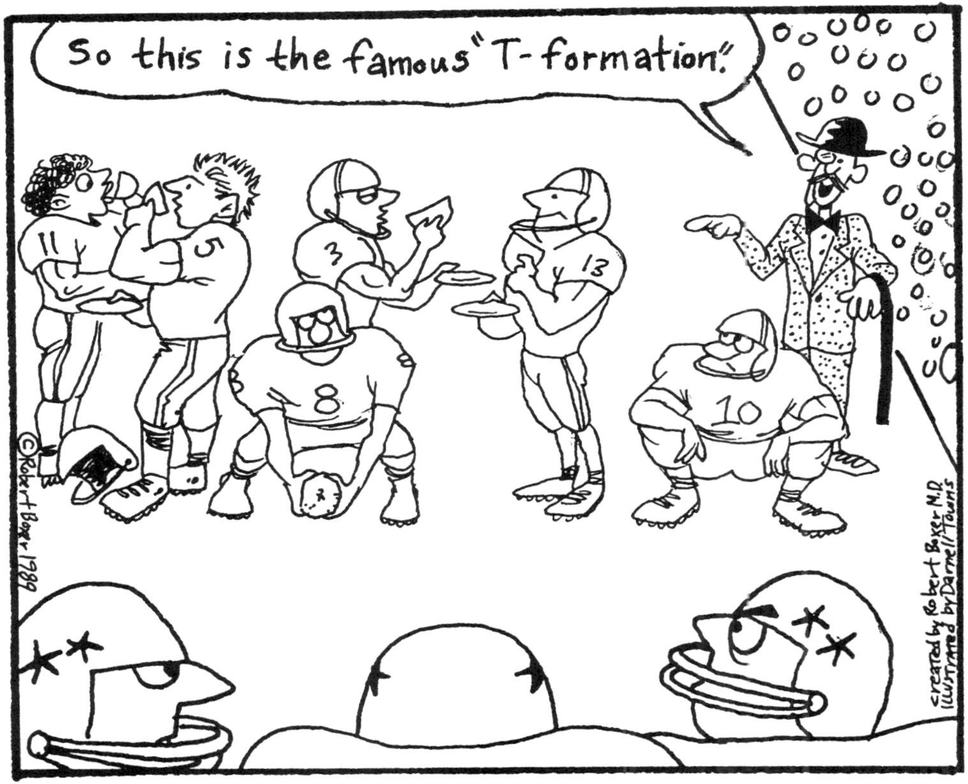
So this is the famous "T-formation."
© Robert Boxer 1989
created by Robert Boxer M.D.
Illustrated by Darnell Towns

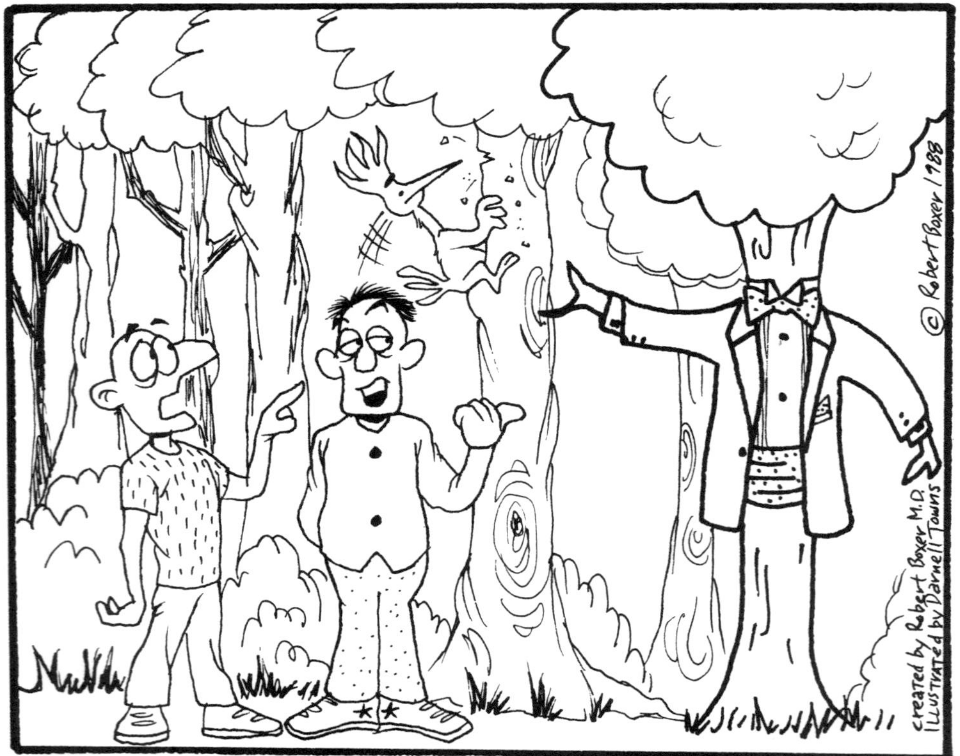
© Robert Boxer 1988
created by Robert Boxer M.D.
ILLUSTRATED by Darnell Towns

LEFT GUY: Why doesn't the Woodpecker peck that particular tree?

RIGHT GUY: Can't you see that tree is dressed impeccably?

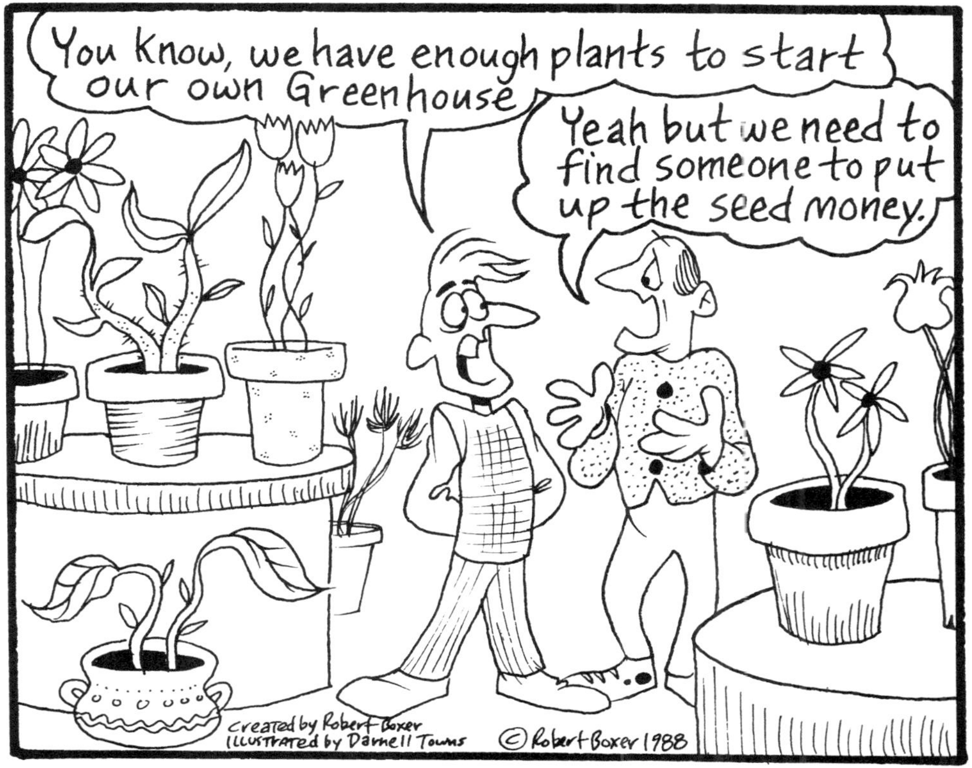
You know, we have enough plants to start our own Greenhouse
Yeah but we need to find someone to put up the seed money.
Created by Robert Boxer
Illustrated by Darnell Towns
© Robert Boxer 1988

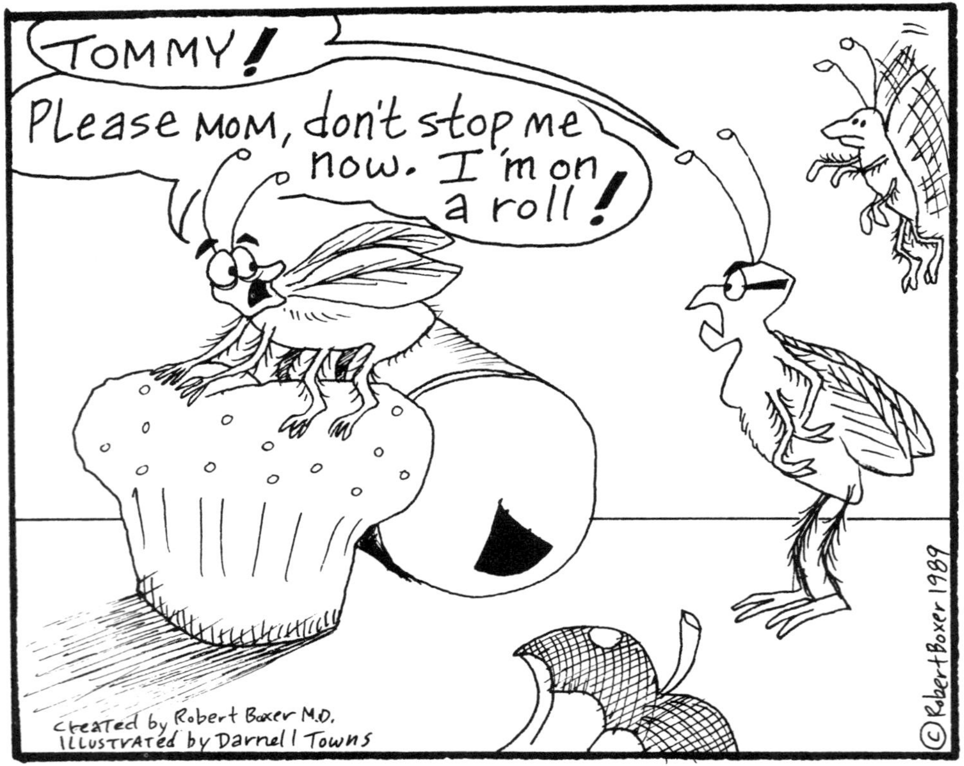
TOMMY!
Please MOM, don't stop me now. I'm on a roll!
Created by Robert Boxer M.D.
Illustrated by Darnell Towns
© Robert Boxer 1989

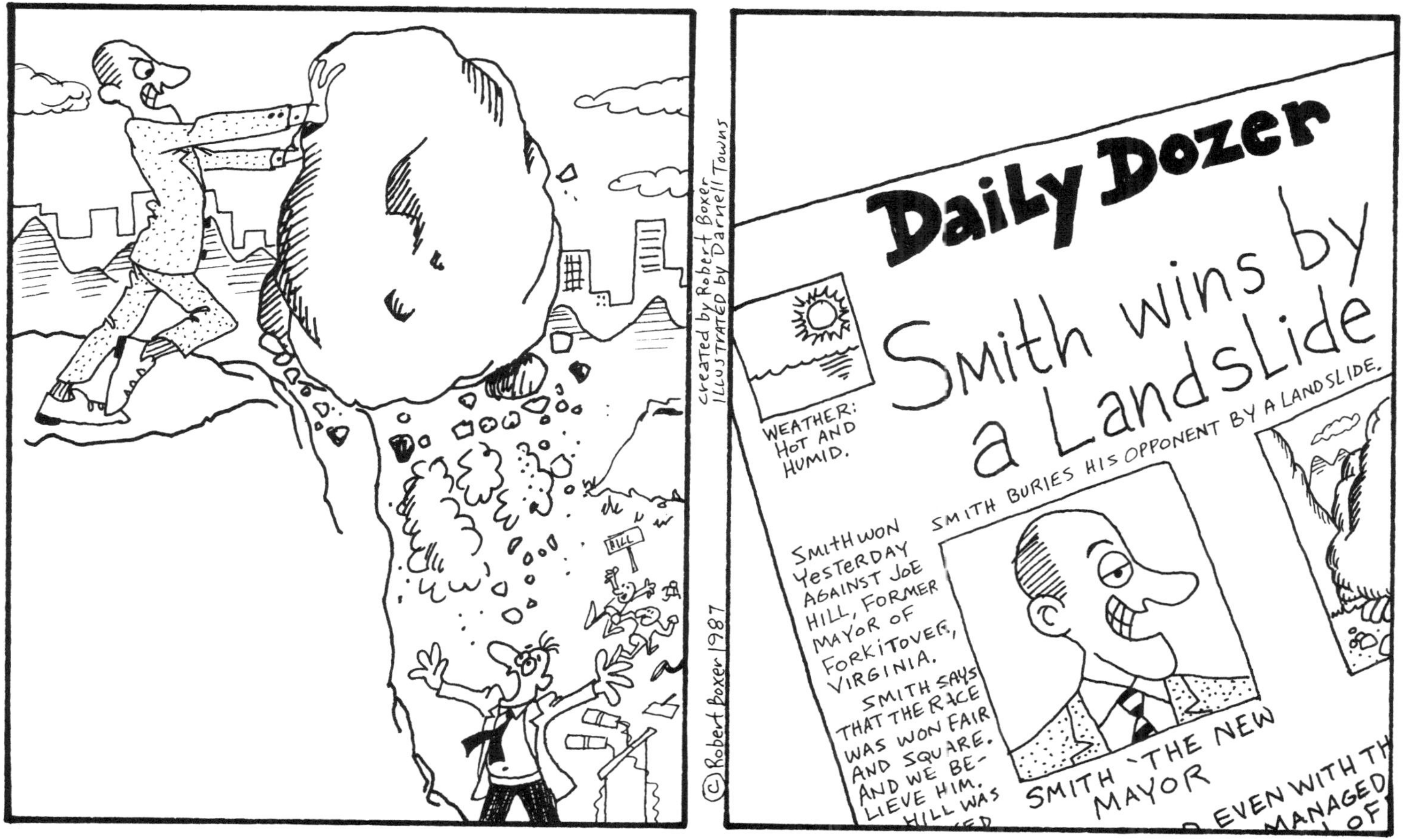
HILL
created by Robert Boxer
ILLUSTRATED by Darnell Towns
© Robert Boxer 1987
Daily Dozer
Smith wins by a LandsLide
WEATHER: HOT AND HUMID.
SMITH BURIES HIS OPPONENT BY A LANDSLIDE.
SMITH WON YESTERDAY AGAINST JOE HILL, FORMER MAYOR OF FORKITOVER, VIRGINIA.
SMITH SAYS THAT THE RACE WAS WON FAIR AND SQUARE. AND WE BELIEVE HIM.
SMITH 'THE NEW MAYOR

"Two dollars for a massage!? Okay.... ....where's the RuB?!"

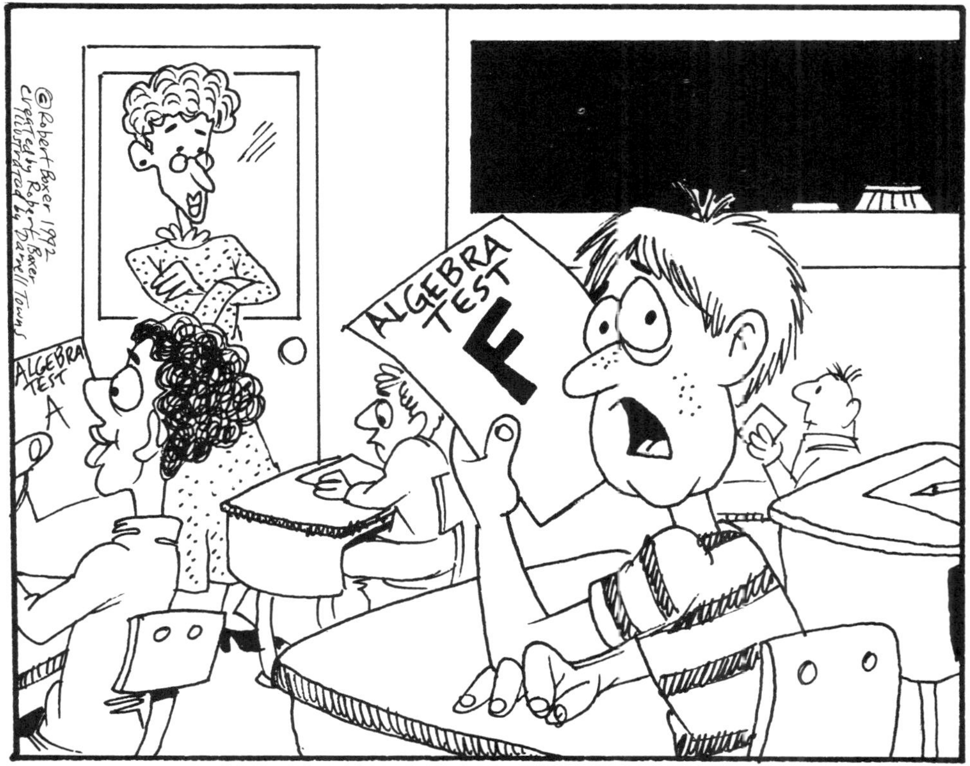

© Robert Baxter 1992
created by Robert Baxter
Illustrated by Darrell Towns
ALGEBRA TEST A
ALGEBRA TEST F

"There must be a HIGHER POWER that I can appeal to."

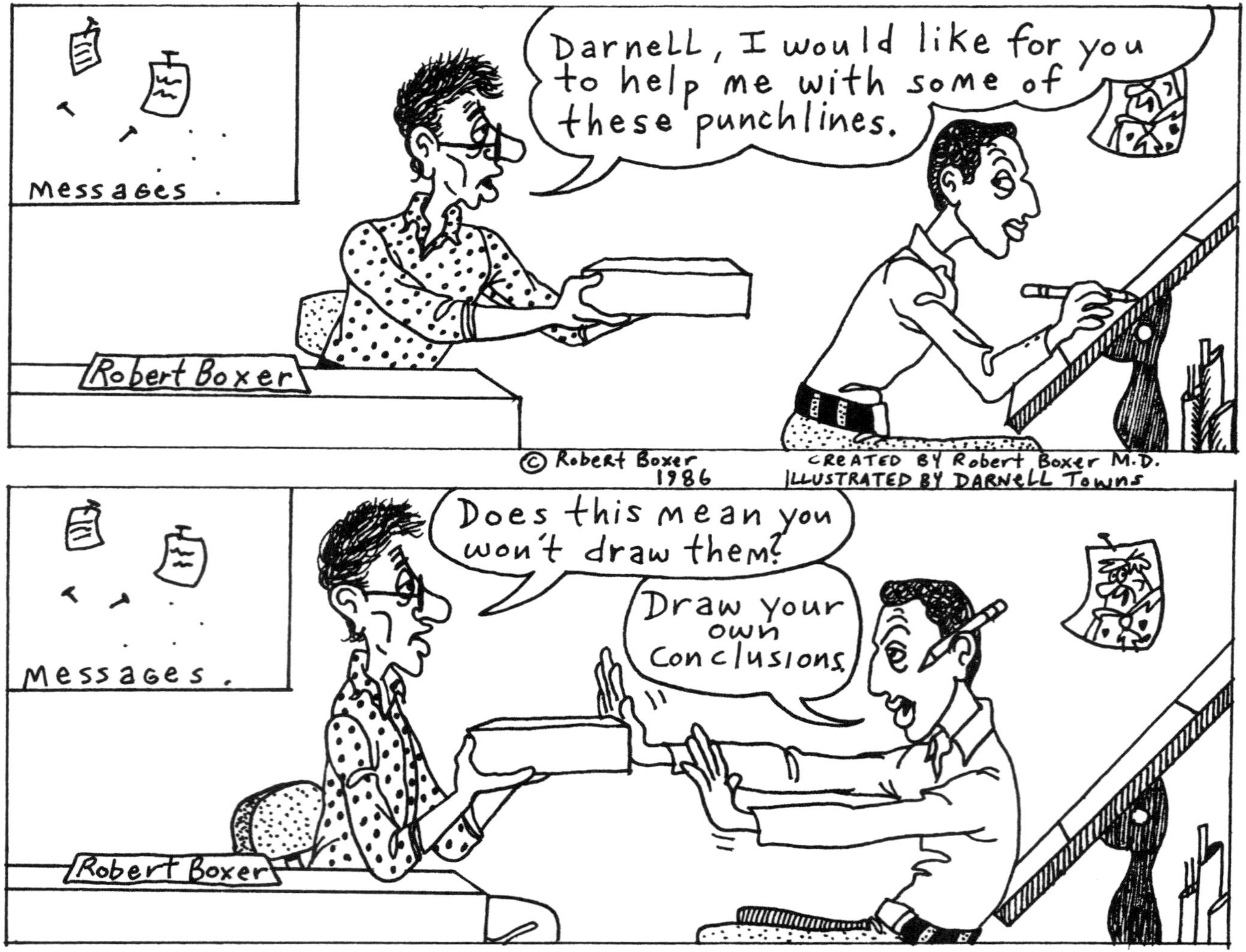
Messages.
Darnell, I would like for you to help me with some of these punchlines.
Robert Boxer
© Robert Boxer 1986
CREATED BY Robert Boxer M.D.
ILLUSTRATED BY DARNELL Towns
Messages.
Does this mean you won't draw them?
Draw your own conclusions.
Robert Boxer

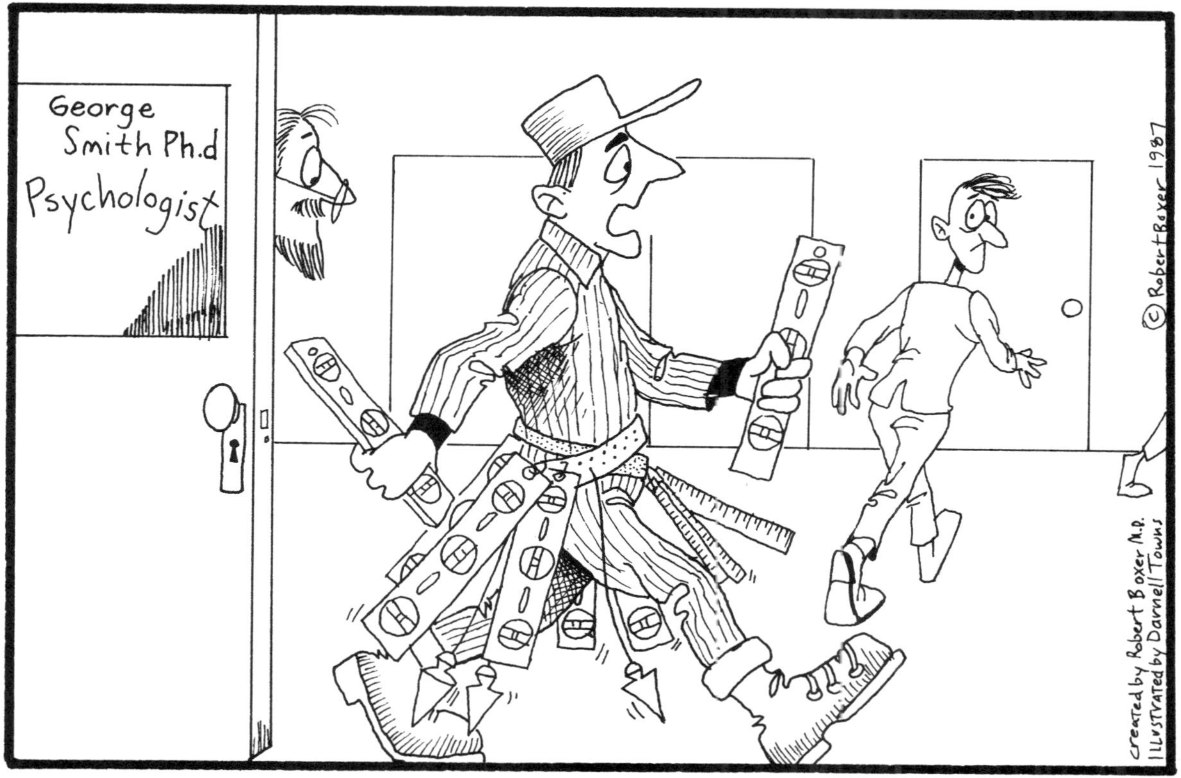
George
Smith Ph.d
Psychologist
© Robert Boxer 1987
created by Robert Boxer M.D.
ILLUSTRATED by Darnell Towns

"I wonder why Dr. Smith said I'm too **self-centered**".

"Ok, Ok, I'll tell you. Charlie Bambino Crow did it on the Statue in the park, Harry Horwitz Hawk did it on your open convertible, and Ricardo Robin took care of your new uniform. That's all I know."

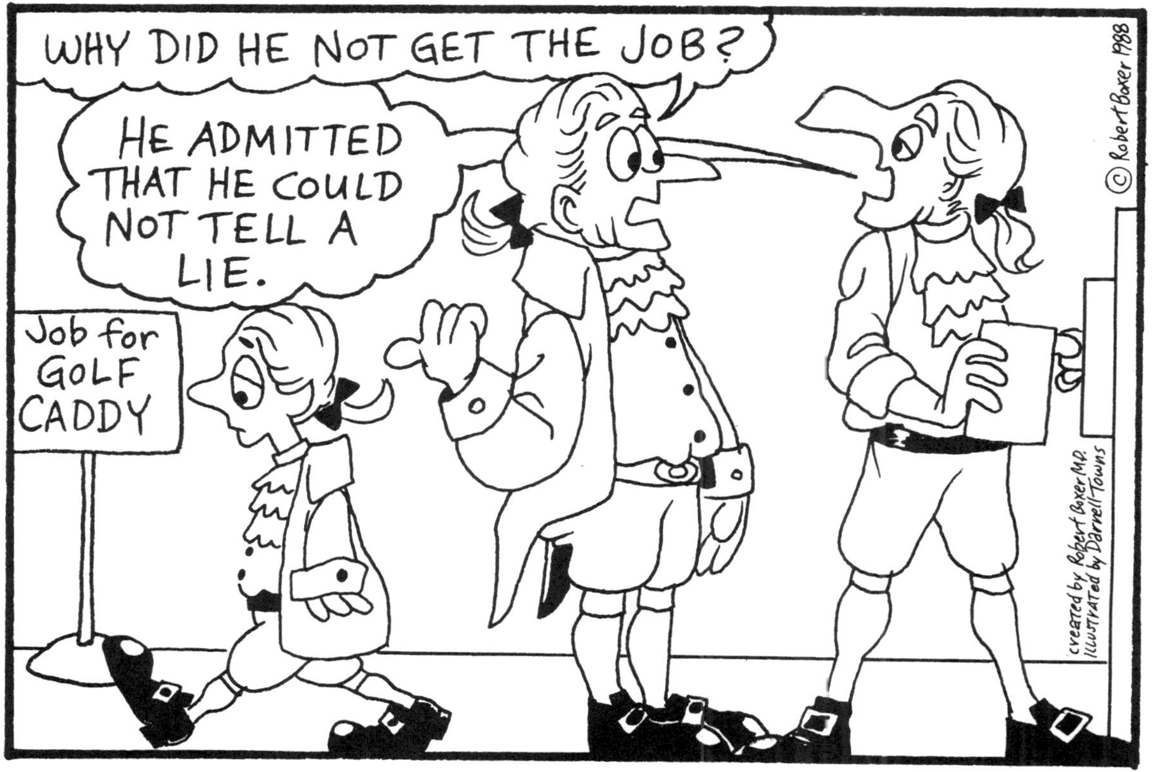
WHY DID HE NOT GET THE JOB?
HE ADMITTED THAT HE COULD NOT TELL A LIE.
Job for GOLF CADDY
© Robert Boxer 1988
created by Robert Boxer M.D.
illustrated by Darrell Towns

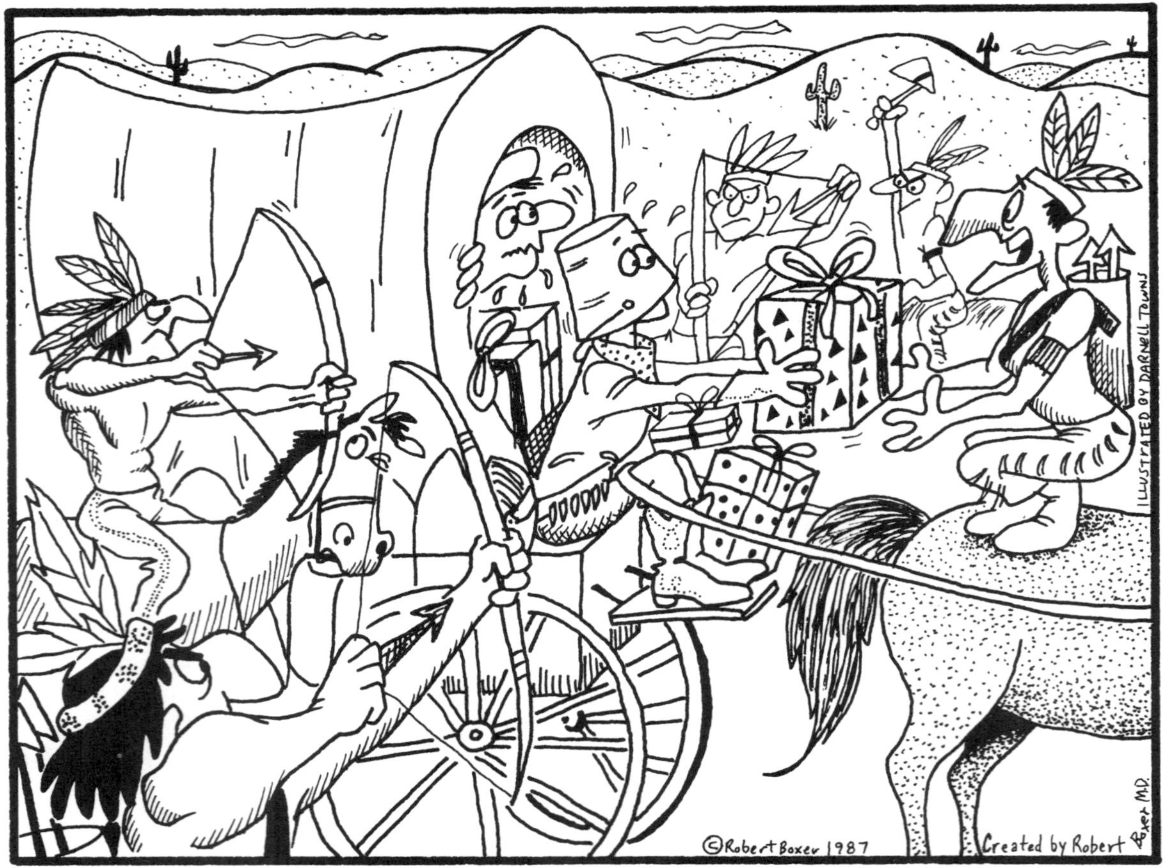
ILLUSTRATED BY DARNELL TOWNS
©Robert Boxer 1987
Created by Robert Boxer M.D.

"Pail face has good stage presents".

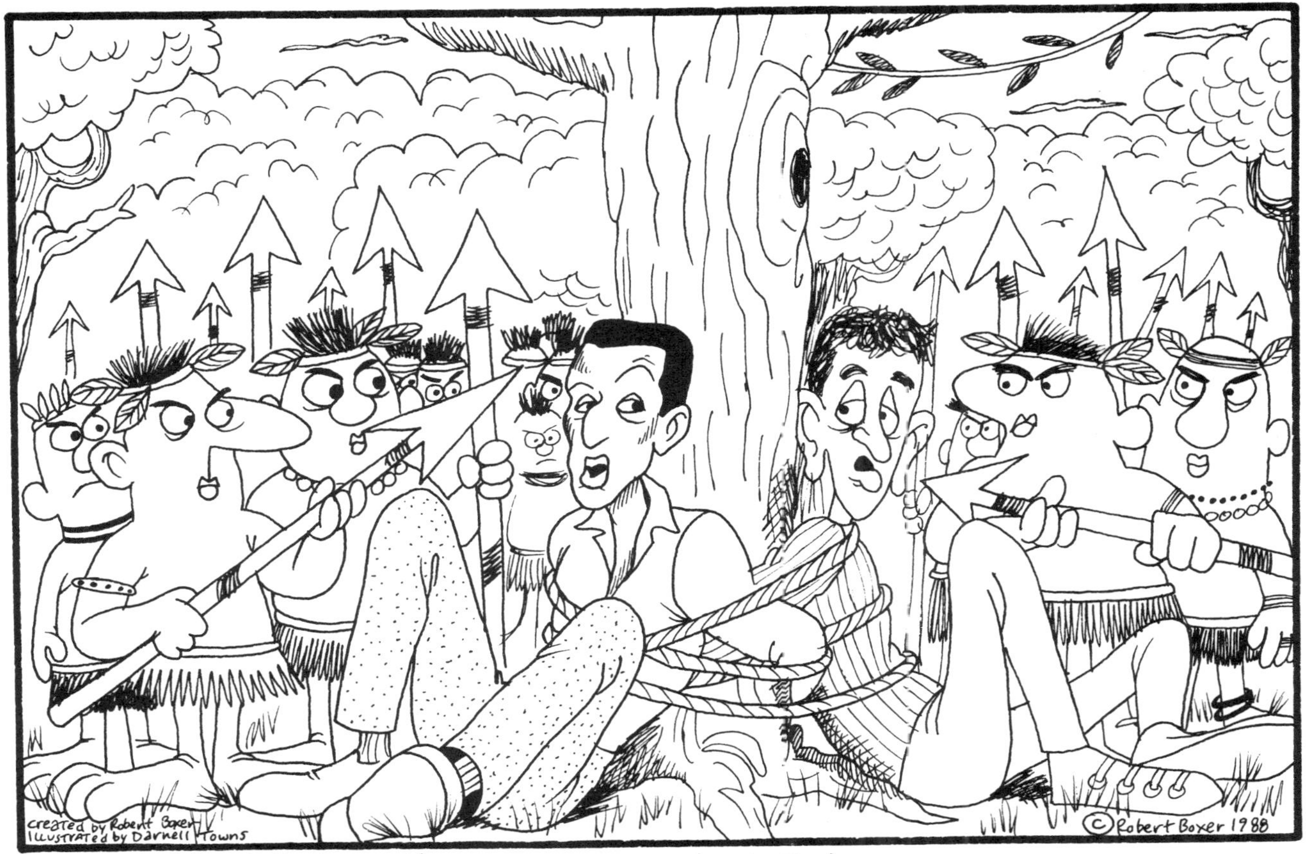
created by Robert Boxer
Illustrated by Darnell Towns
©Robert Boxer 1988

DARNELL: "Bob, tell some puns; that'll drive anyone away."
BOB: "I'm trying, Darnell, but they're all going over their heads."

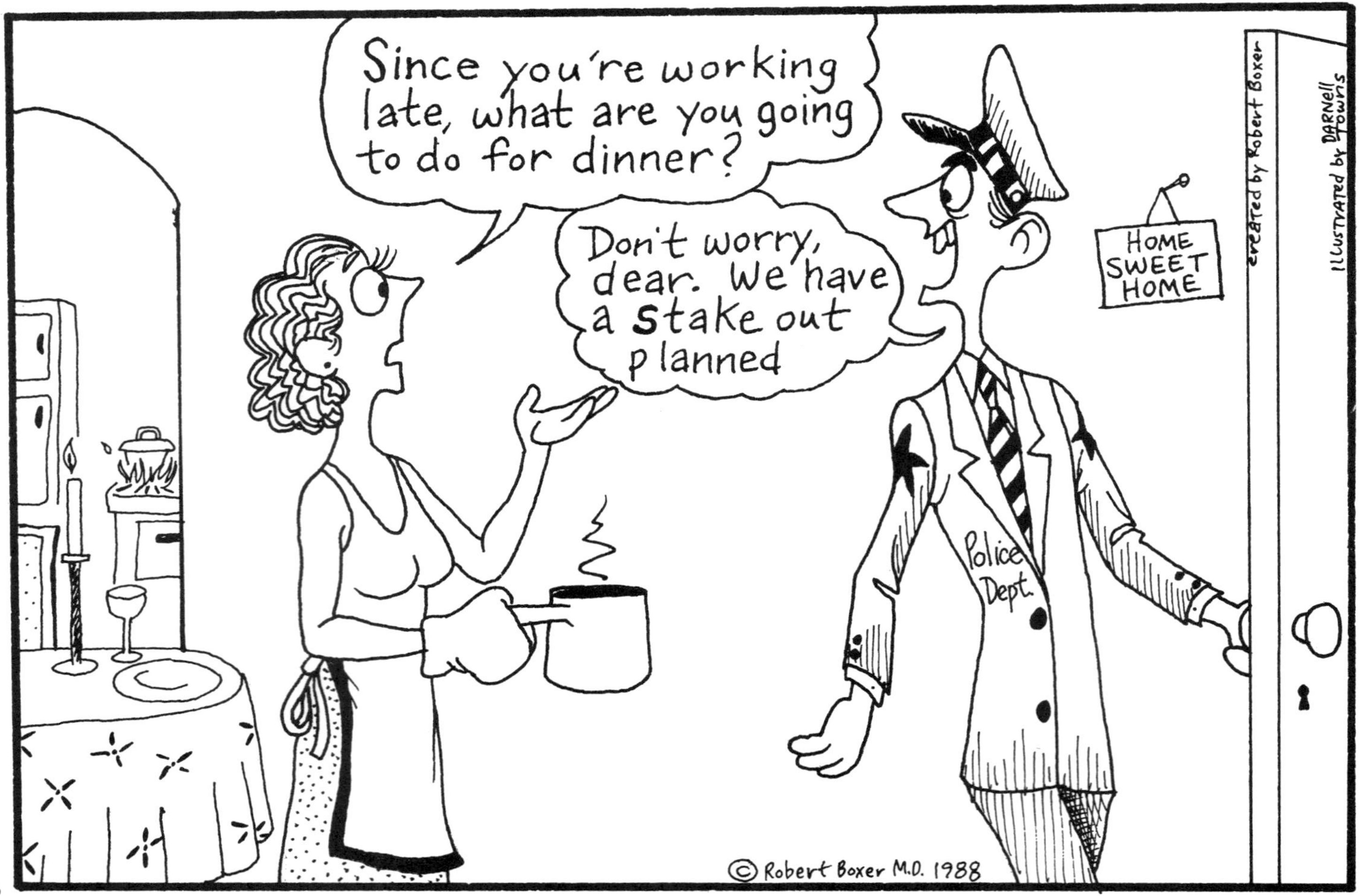
Since you're working late, what are you going to do for dinner?
Don't worry, dear. We have a stake out planned
HOME SWEET HOME
Police Dept.
created by Robert Boxer
Illustrated by DARNELL TOWNS
© Robert Boxer M.D. 1988

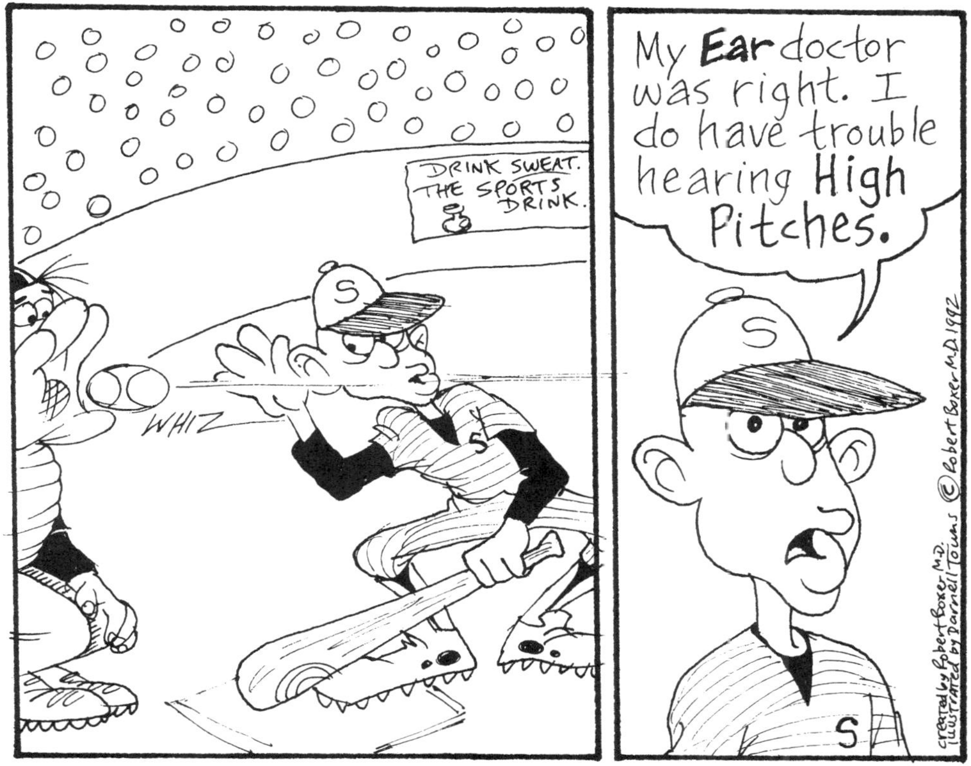
DRINK SWEAT. THE SPORTS DRINK.
WHIZ
My Ear doctor was right. I do have trouble hearing High Pitches.
created by Robert Boxer M.D.
ILLUSTRATED by Darnell Towns
© Robert Boxer M.D. 1992

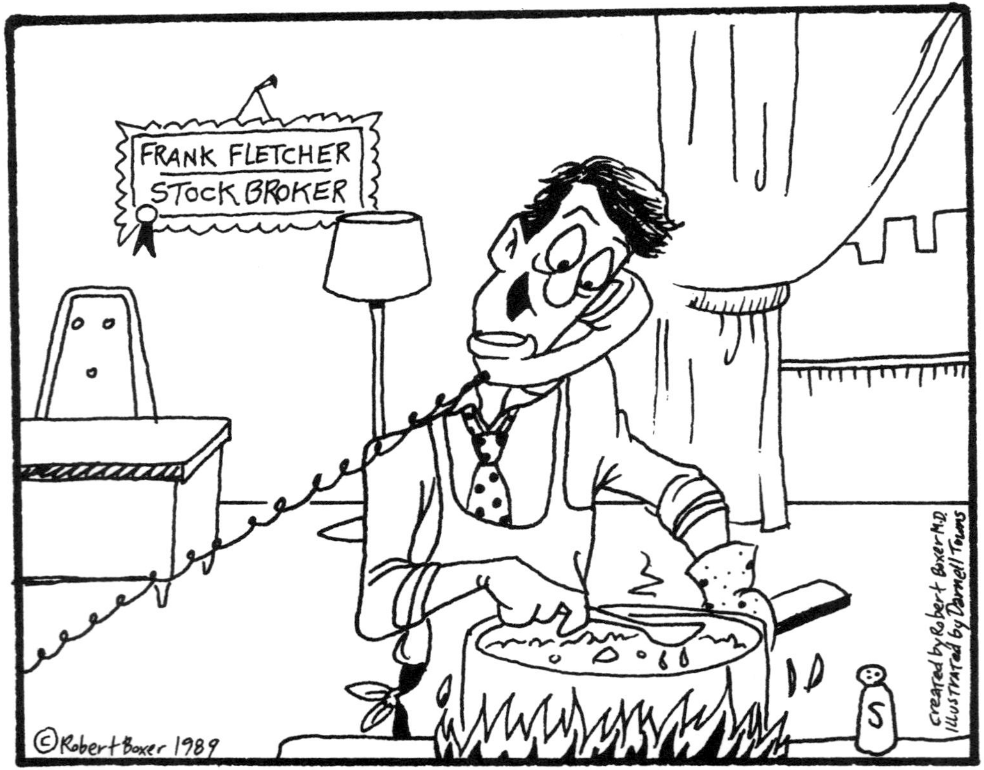
FRANK FLETCHER
STOCK BROKER
S
©Robert Boxer 1989
created by Robert Boxer M.D.
illustrated by Darnell Towns

"Hello?....Mr. Kramer? Hi, I wanted to call you right away. I think I've found a great soupstock."

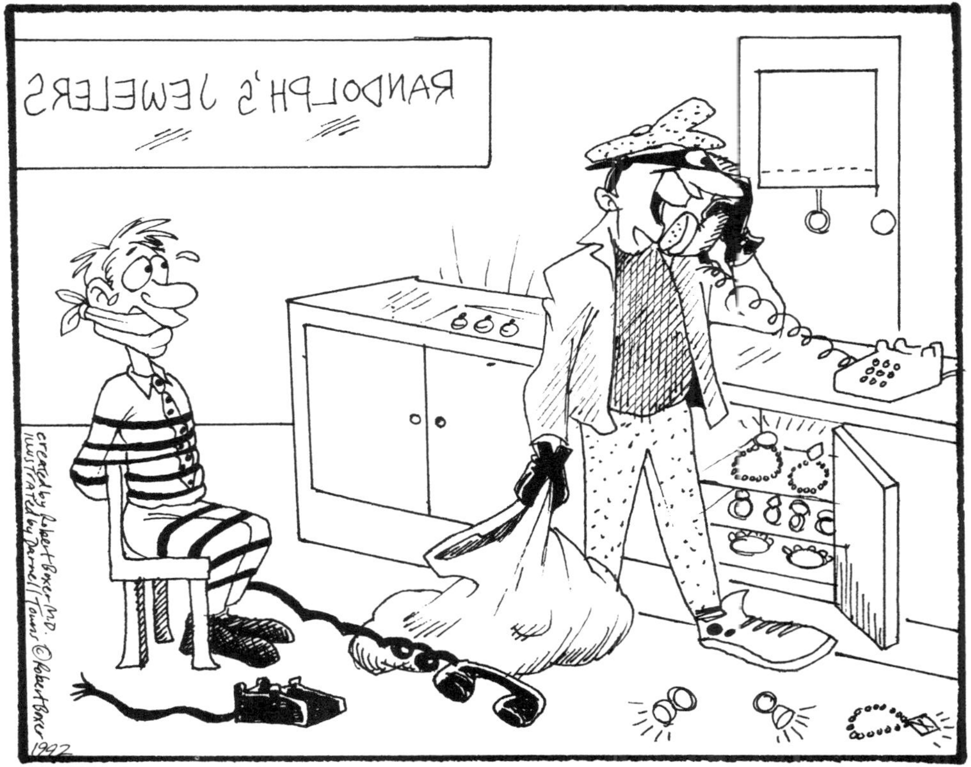
RANDOLPH'S JEWELERS
created by Robert Boxer M.D.
ILLUSTRATED by Darrell Towns © Robert Boxer 1992

"Mr. Randolph is tied up with the other line, can I take a message?"

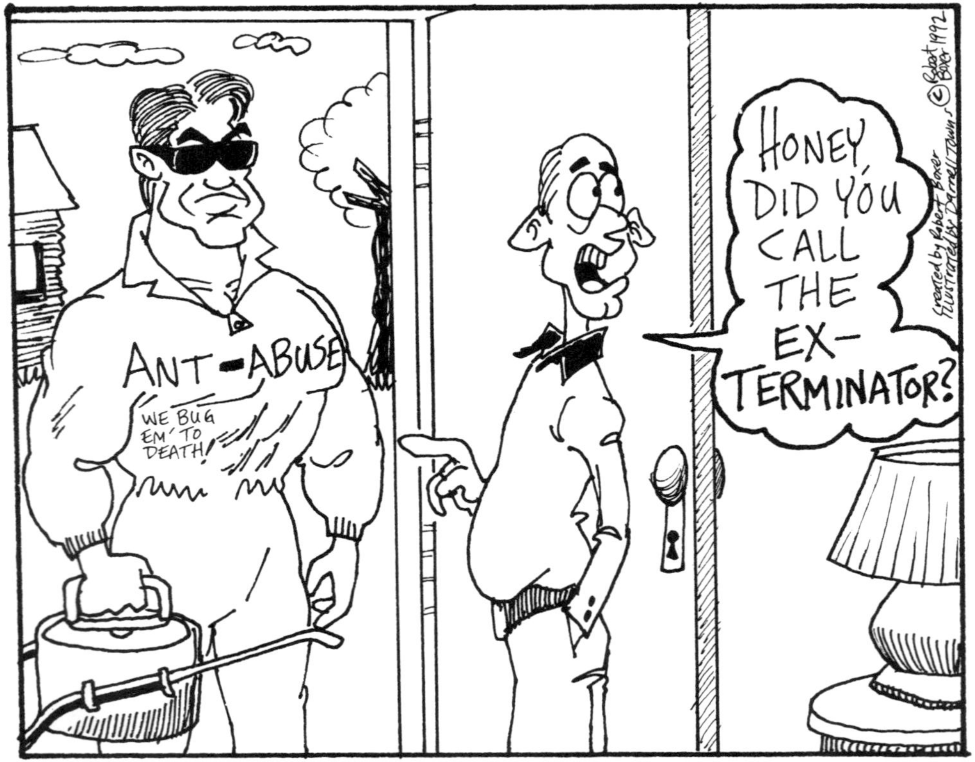
ANT-ABUSE
WE BUG EM' TO DEATH!
HONEY, DID YOU CALL THE EX-TERMINATOR?
Created by Robert Boxer
Illustrated by Darnell Towns
© Robert Boxer 1992

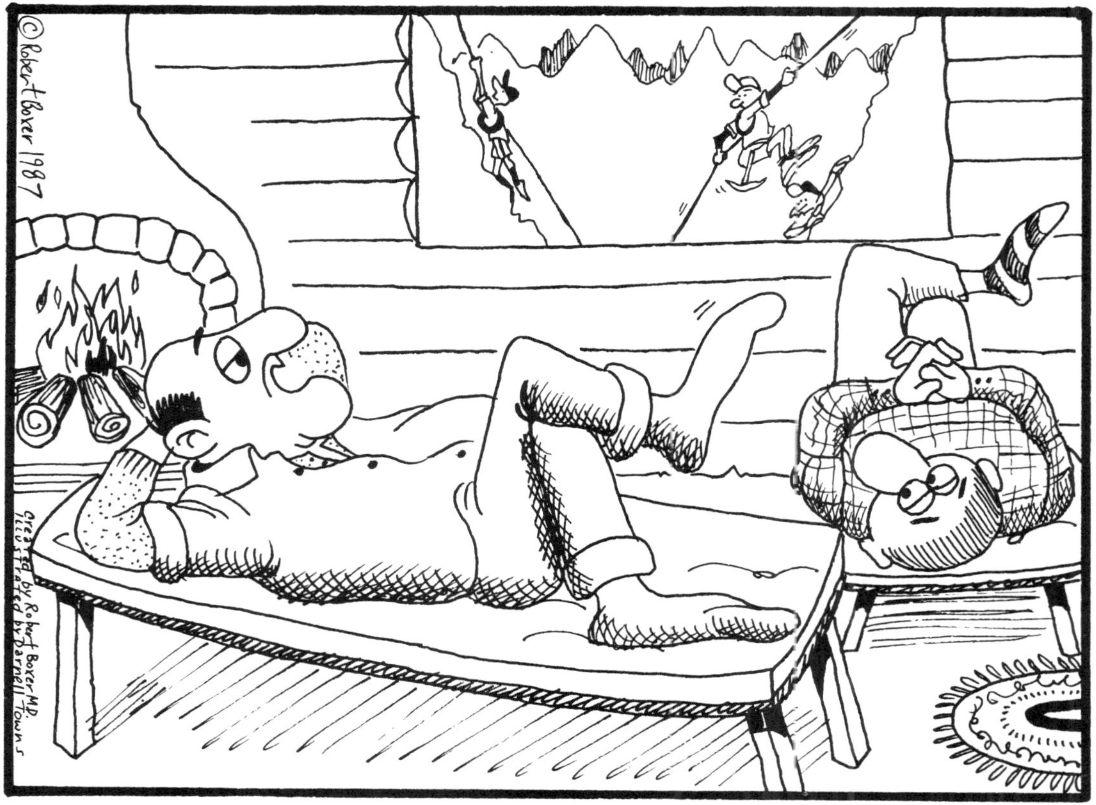
© Robert Boxer 1987
Created by Robert Boxer M.D.
Illustrated by Darnell Towns

"The very thought of climbing mountains is rappelling to me."

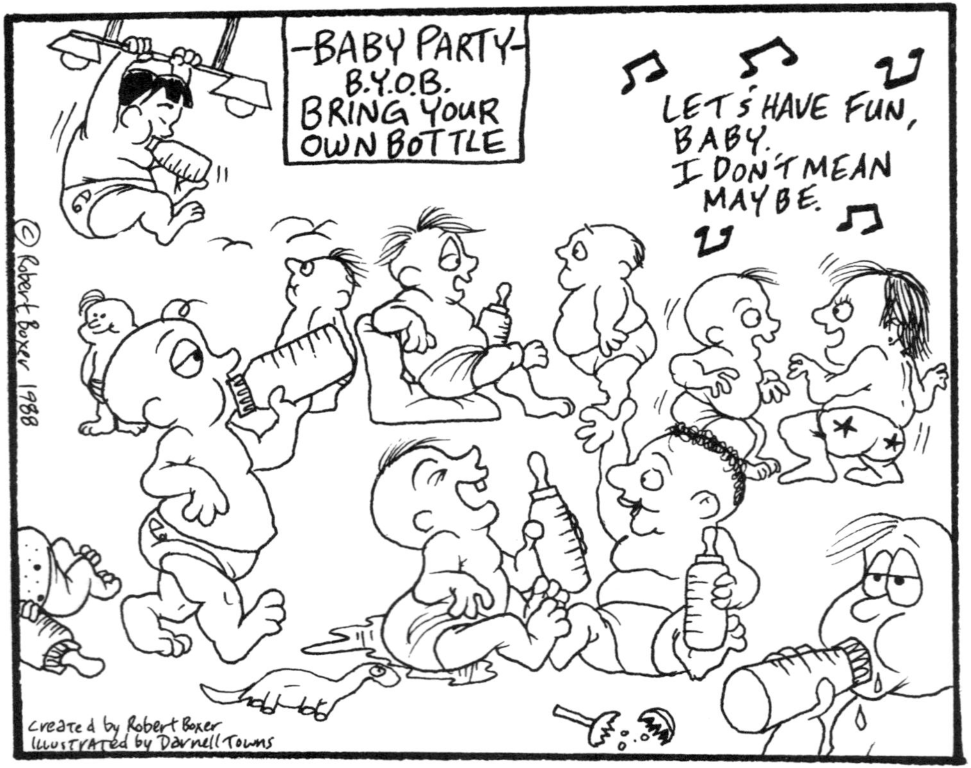
-BABY PARTY-
B.Y.O.B.
BRING YOUR
OWN BOTTLE
LET'S HAVE FUN,
BABY.
I DON'T MEAN
MAYBE.
© Robert Boxer 1988
created by Robert Boxer
Illustrated by Darnell Towns

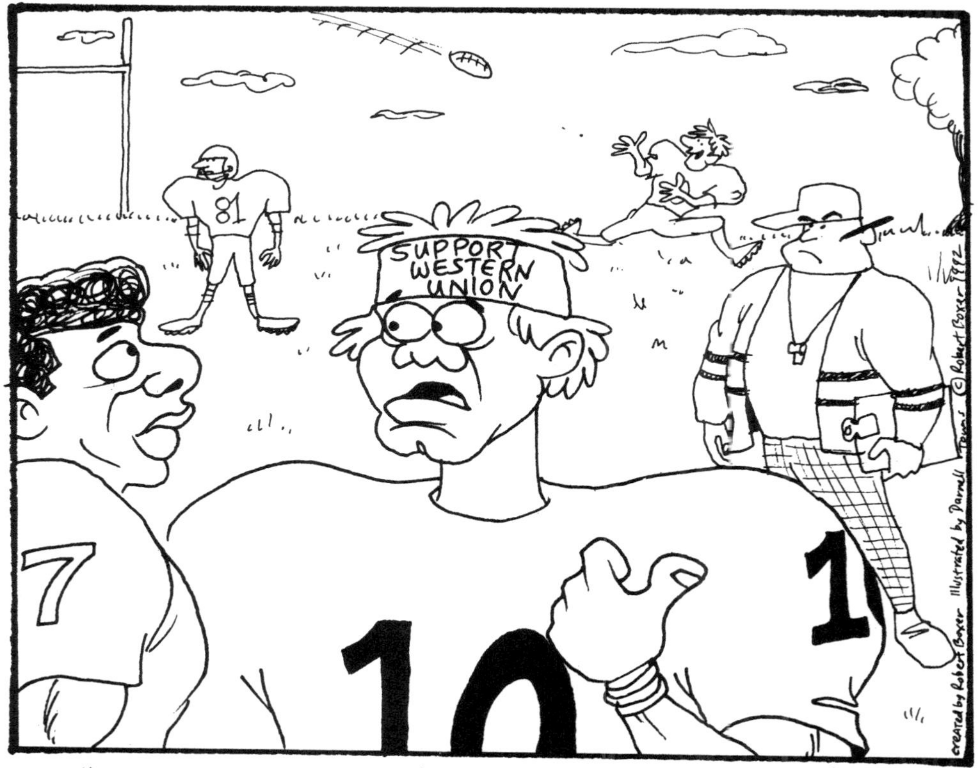
SUPPORT WESTERN UNION
81
7
10
created by Robert Boxer Illustrated by Darrell Evans © Robert Boxer 1992

"I wonder why the coach is worried that I might **telegraph** my passes."

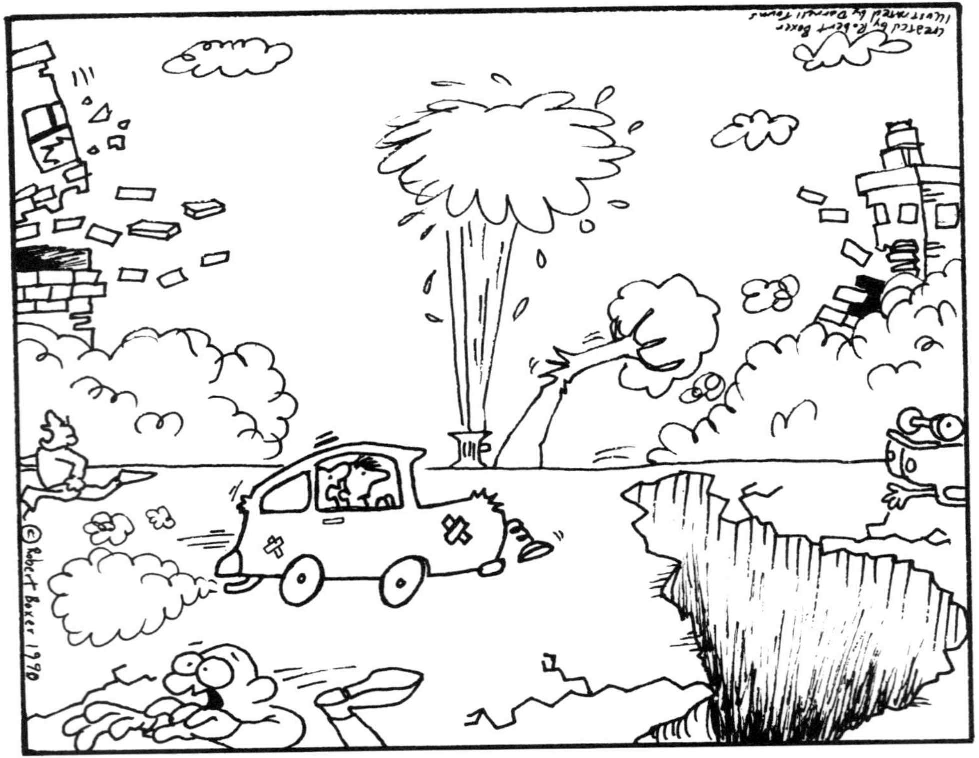
created by Robert Boxer
illustrated by Darrell Towns
© Robert Boxer 1990

PASSENGER: "Are you going to drive this car into the **ground**?"
DRIVER: "Yes, but through no **FAULT** of my own."

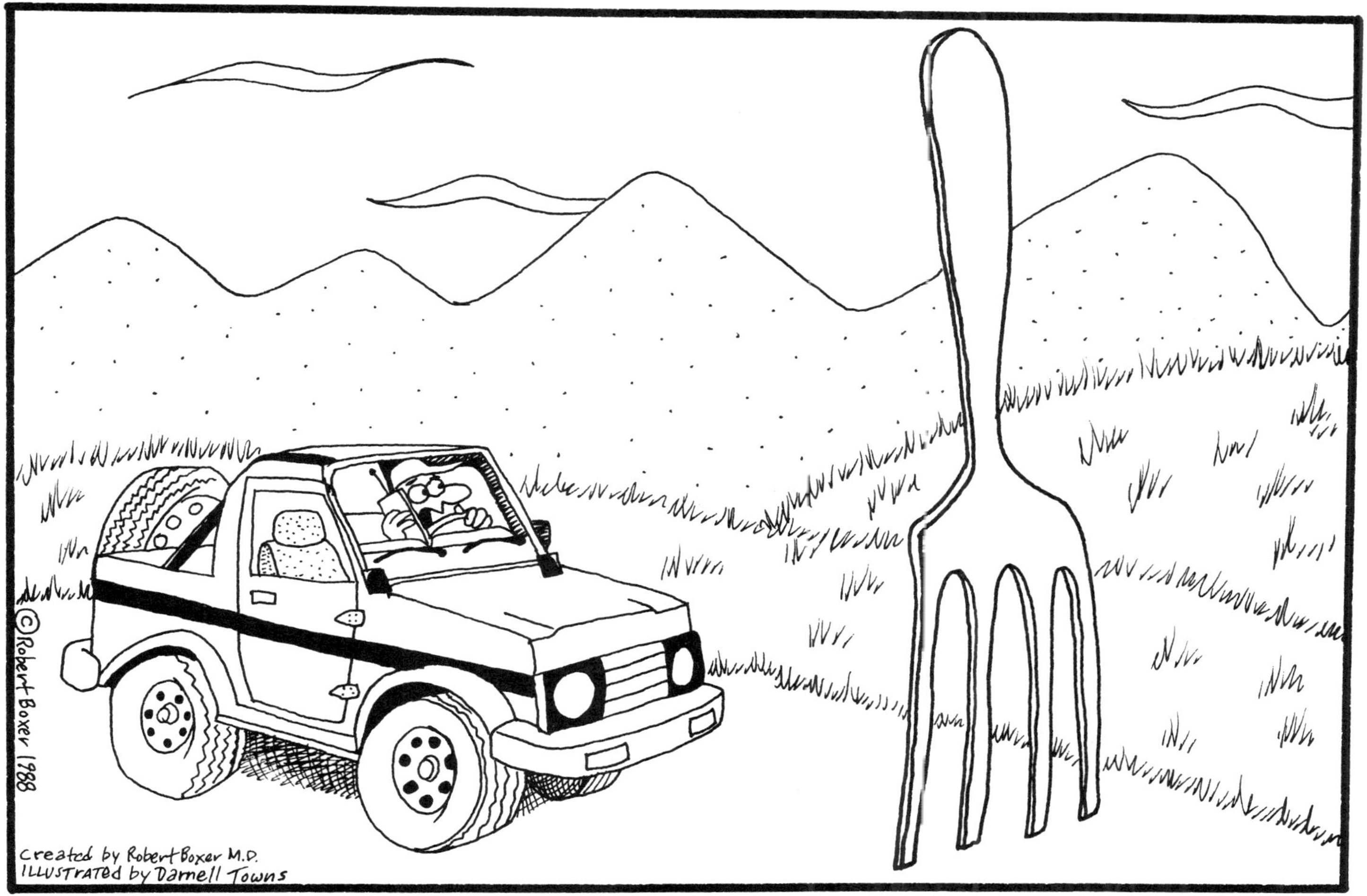
© Robert Boxer 1988
created by Robert Boxer M.D.
ILLUSTRATED by Darnell Towns

"I think I've come to a fork in the road".

Acknowledgements
(The Guilty Parties)

For encouragement and support of the creative ? process that led to this collection of pun cartoons, I am especially indebted to: friends Bill and Zehavah Frankel for painstakingly (and I suspect painfully) reviewing all of the cartoons. Bill is a copyright attorney, and his and Zehavah's advice have been invaluable ; Jody Yeh, a friend and very clever punster, who also reviewed all the cartoons, and made creative suggestions; Carole Isaacs, our copy editor, who also gave me valuable feedback on all of the cartoons; and Nancy Janus who typed many of the cartoons and made comments and helpful suggestions.

Additionally, support and encouragement, both past and present were provided by a multitude of colleagues, relatives and friends including the following: Doctors Eugene Goldman, Wayne Wirtz, Renee Reich, Lenny Berlin, Larry Maillis (a virtual auricle -- pun intended -- of information both trivial and significant), Herb Lipschultz, Arnie Swerdlow, Michael Lewis, Ray Hechter, Arkady Rapoport, Harold Laker, Sushil Sharma, Abe Chervony, Leigh Rosenblum, Gary Novetsky, Mort Doblin, Bernie Hankin, David Lee, Saeed Khan, Pat Ebenhoeh, Joe LaMothe, Naphtali Gutstein, Alan Pollak, Ray Firfer, Harry Goldin, Alon Winnie, Myles Cunningham, Jonathan Berlin, Coley Seskind, Marty Kaplan, Stephen Lippitz, Steven Fischman, Tom Stone, Gary Oberg, Allan Lieberman, William Rea, Del Stigler, Cliff Brooks, Mort Teich, Frank Waickman, Wayne Konetzki, Bill Kerr, Jim Holland, Jake Suker, Jerry Haase, Dave Fretzin, Charlie Swarts (the fastest pun in the west and my former

teacher), Seymour Gottlieb, Bill Fagman, Paul Bubala, Larry Elegant, Marianne Budzeika, Gene and Joan Meyer, Abraham and Molly Jacob, Suellyn Rossman, Robert LaPata, Herb Greenfield, Don Kozil, Steve Adams, Jerry Zoot, Jerold Miller, Kenneth Krischer, George Burica, Doris Rapp, Jerry Bernstein, and Stuart Meyer.

Also Shelly and Elliott Abramson, Ann Marie Pryde, Verne Bengtson, Jim and Carolyn Snorek, Bob and Estelle Katz, Esther Berg, Jack and Helen Boxer, Eric Boxer, Russell Boxer (my Godson and heir apparent punster), Martin and Lucille Boxer, Lois Gartenberg, Rose Levin (my mother-in-law), Aunt Mary Neman, Martin and Helen Boxer, Phil and Florine Boxer, Michael and Frada Boxer, Joyce Heitler, the unbelievably clever and creative punster and organizer of the highly successful Annual Punsters Dinner in Chicago, George Pattison, former editor of *The Main Event, Monthly Sports Journal for Physicians,* Gail Krischer, Howard and Sheila Pizer, David, Janet, Steve, and Brian Altman, Myrtie Jane Kreutzer, Beatrice Trum Hunter, Marjorie Hurt Jones, Judy Bartuch, Marge Tepperman, Joe Bobak, Joe Bobak, Jr., Tom Kretler, John Eisenbart, Ed Hult, Barbara Sachsel, Chris Moriarity-Field and Mark Field, Bob and Judy Silverforb, Diane Oeste, Ken and Charlotte Levy, Fred and Jackie Mayer, Penni Berman, Ron Siegel, Anita Siegel, Mel and Dee Dee Evenson, Harold Bosmann, Sol Bloom, LeRoy Kwiatt, Howard Weinert, Barbara Kravets, Bonnie Minsky, Eulalia Adam, Judy West, Anshel Gostomelsky, Ricky and Bobbi Litt, Suzanne Litt, Sam and Amy Rabin,

Jack and Joni Hartman, Bob and Sandra Silver, Tony Placzek, Marcia Placzek, Carol Hopwood, Karen Eness, Vivian VanBrundt, Gwen Ott, Jack Isaacs, Andrew Fisher, Marjorie Fisher, Evelyn Winfield, Bud and Georgia Photopulos, Scott and Camille Lewis, Linda Forman, Jack and Fran Mabley, Don Ziegler, June Winnie, Phyllis Berlin, Judy Kaplan, Alan Finger, Avery DeLott, David Hochman, Nick Mechales, Gene Goldberg, Larry and Helen Levine, Jack and Judy Wortell, Gary and Sue Boxer, Darren Miller, Marshall Cordell, an inveterate punster and successful entrepreneur, Joe Sugarman, also a successful entrepreneur, author, and speaker, Gary, Karyn, Marcy, and Alan Gilbert, Morrie and Rhoda Dubinsky, John Yeh, Aunt Zelda Silverforb, Bob and Susan Flappan, Marc and Barbara Birnbaum, Ed and Lisa Stein, Aunt Anna Keller, Mary Buckley, Diane Plennert, Grace Holt, Susan Jahnke, Lynn Beran, Linda Balogh, Barbara Mussen, Marci Good, Pat Healy, Cathy Artman, Iris Gottlieb, Dick Boylan, Jim Sanders of Chapter One, and Ray Carroll.

Especially supportive have been: Bob Herguth, columnist for the Chicago Sun-Times, Jim Frankenbach, president of Rush North Shore Medical Center, Ord Matek, A.C.S.W., an author and neighbor, and cousin Jack Boxer.

To all of these dear and fine people, and to all those inadvertently omitted, I am deeply appreciative of your support and encouragement, but please remember that you are all guilty of aiding and abetting a punster!

About the Author

Dr. Robert W. Boxer is a practicing allergist, with offices in the Professional Building of the Old Orchard Center in Skokie, Illinois, a suburb of Chicago. Bob has created thousands of pun cartoons, and many have been illustrated by Darnell Towns. For four years, pun cartoons incorporating the themes of medicine and sports appeared regularly in *The Main Event, Monthly Sports Journal for Physicians.* Bob's first book, *Boxer's Shorts, More than just a Brief attempt at Humor,* also illustrated by Darnell Towns, was published in 1988. After graduating from Southwest High School in Kansas City, Missouri, Bob earned his pre-medical degree at the University of Denver. He then obtained his medical degree from Northwestern University Medical School, served his internship and residency at Cook County Hospital in Chicago, and trained in allergy at the University of Illinois College of Medicine in Chicago. Currently, he is on the medical staffs of Lutheran General Hospital in Park Ridge, Illinois, and Rush North Shore Medical Center in Skokie, Illinois. He is a fellow of the American Academy of Allergy and Immunology, the American College of Allergy and Immunology, the American Association of Board Certified Allergists, the Illinois Society of Allergy and Immunology, and the American Academy of Environmental Medicine. He is a member of the American Medical Association and the Illinois State and Chicago Medical Societies. Dr. Boxer is on the Professional Advisory Board of the "Nutrition for Optimal Health Association", and is a member of Alpha Omega Alpha, Honor Medical Society He is a member of "The International Save the Pun Foundation", and was named Punster of the Year by this foundation, in 1993.

About the Illustrator

Darnell Towns graduated from The School of the Art Institute of Chicago, with a B.F.A. in Filmmaking and Animation. Born and raised on Chicago's South side, Darnell began drawing at an early age. He attended Wendell Phillip's High School, where he excelled in his art classes.

Currently, Mr. Towns is freelancing as an animator and a caricaturist. His works have been exhibited at various museums and galleries. He has collaborated with Dr. Boxer for the past nine years illustrating a series of *BOXER'S SHORTS*.

List of Cartoons

1. Did Have A Reservation?
2. On A Higher Plane
3. Travel Logs
4. Goodbye Mr. Chips
5. Sox And Orioles
6. Flying The Coop
7. Comic Relief
8. Cut A Dill
9. Maps In The Trunk
10. Winner Of Spelling Bee
11. Middle Of A Sentence
12. Crab To Lobster
13. For A Credit Card
14. Heroine Bust
15. Opportunity To Unwind
16. Cartoons Are Tasteless
17. Dual Citizenship
18. Shooting The Breeze
19. Piece Of Cake
20. Best Cellar List
21. Art Of Scrambling
22. Bus Boy
23. Shining Sea
24. Redemption Fee
25. Cell Of The Century
26. Boarding School
27. Up And Down Career
28. Echo System
29. Kill Roaches
30. Big Buck Spending
31. Judge A Suit
32. Couped Up
33. Call A Fencer
34. Bleachers
35. French Impressionists
36. Dummy Corporations
37. Difficult For Seeds
38. Nothing Beneath Her
39. Food And Spirits
40. Liquidation Sale
41. Permanent Aisle Seat
42. Faith In Bible
43. Setting A Screen
44. Log Cabin
45. Another Log Cabbin
46. Royal Flush
47. Black Sheep
48. Ghost Writers
49. Bare Aspirin
50. Photography Studio
51. Pyramid Scheme
52. Stalemate
53. Puntunes
54. Poor Taste

55. Bare Arms
56. Holy Mackerel
57. Autobiographies
58. 25" Screen
59. Train Of Thought
60. Bullet Proof Glass Company
61. Roaches Multiply
62. Overboard For Blondes
63. Collecting Credit Cards
64. Highest Resolution
65. Small Cobbler
66. Through The Grapevine
67. Light Year
68. Sleep Last Night
69. Double Dip
70. U-All Rentals
71. Catch Up Football
72. Illegally Parked Fans
73. Quarter Horse
74. Rye Humor
75. Pamper Yourself
76. News In Depth
77. Wide Receiver
78. Sick Bat Boy
79. Cattle Drive
80. Too Pooped
81. No Shoe Horns
82. Cross Examination
83. Out Of The Gun
84. Zero Drop Out Rate
85. Down Payment
86. Chips For Dipping
87. Pro-Bowler
88. Fish Get Hooked
89. Carpenter Ants
90. Ferret Yourself
91. Heir Rifle
92. Sleeper In Race
93. Knight School
94. "Fish Bowl"
95. Against All Odds
96. Racist
97. Catch-Up Sleep
98. Zip Codes
99. T-Formation
100. Dressed Impeccably
101. Seed Money
102. On A Roll
103. Wins By Landslide
104. Massage
105. Higher Power
106. Draw Conclusions
107. Too Self-Centered
108. Stool Pidgeon

109. Golf Caddy Job
110. Good Stage Presents
111. Puns Over Heads
112. Stake Out Planned
113. High Pitches
114. Great Soup Stock
115. Tied Up With Other Line
116. Ex-Terminator
117. Climbing Mountains
118. BYOB Party
119. Telegraph Passes
120. Drive Car Into Ground
121. Fork In The Road

Book Order Form

**Attention:
Schools and Businesses**

Punchline Press™ books are available at quantity discounts with bulk purchase for educational, business, or sales promotional use. For information, Please write to Special Sales Dept., Punchline Press, Box 6058, Wilmette, IL 60091

BOXER'S SHORTS (More Than Just a Brief Attempt at Humor) **ROUND 2**
This book is available at fine book stores, or by sending $9.95, plus $2.50 to cover postage and handling, (add $1 for postage and handling for each additional book), to the following address: Punchline Press. P.O. Box 6058, Wilmette, Illinois 60091

Please send_____books at
$9.95* each $_____

Illinois residents add
8% sales tax $_____

Add $2.50 for shipping and handling for the
first book, add $1.00 for each add'l book $_____

    Total $_____

Check or money order made payable to Punchline Press.

Name_____

Address_____

City_____

State_____

Country_____

Zip Code_____

(Prices subject to change without notice)
Order subject to availability.
Please allow four to six weeks for delivery
All amounts are in U.S. Dollars.

This is a work of fiction. All the characters, situations, and events portrayed in this book are fictional, and any resemblance to real people or incidents is purely coincidental.